TulipTree review

SPRING/SUMMER 2023
issue #13

Wild Women

TULIPTREE
PUBLISHING, LLC

Contents

Life on the Ledge

Amy Soscia

THE BEEPING SOUND OF A TRUCK BACKING UP UNDER HER WINDOW CAPTURED Ruby's attention. She looked outside and watched as the driver tried to squeeze his extra-long moving truck into the only parking space on the street. The driver and his two assistants got out to double-check the size of the spot. No. Their truck wouldn't fit.

"I could have told them that," Ruby said aloud.

Someone would have to find the owners of the red car or the black SUV and ask them to move their vehicle.

A tall brunette with a chin-length bob came running up the street. Flashes of red from her high heels, long red cape, and shiny fingernails made Ruby do a double-take. She reminded Ruby of a puppet, with legs like sticks that moved up and down instead of forward and back. The woman argued with the driver, but Ruby couldn't hear them, so she opened her window enough to let the sounds from the outside in, but not so much as to rouse her pigeons from their morning slumber.

Ruby had lived most of her adult life from behind the windows of her fourth-floor walk-up apartment in Greenwich Village and ventured only as far as the trash chute at the end of the hallway or to the building's mailroom. Home is not a prison for most people, but that wasn't true for her. At twenty-nine, she hadn't left the building in years.

She'd been a teenager when she moved in with her grandparents. Grace and Hairy Harry, a pair of rock pigeons, lived on the oversized granite ledges outside of their apartment windows. Charlie and Pip-Squeak eventually joined the flock. Gram had a gentle way of coaxing them into behaving, but that same nurturing ability didn't come naturally to Ruby.

With all the commotion, the pigeons were now awake and demanding their breakfast. Their arrangement was simple. She gave them food and affection, and they gave her love and companionship. Ruby fed them and then turned her attention back to the drama unfolding outside.

Puppet Woman wore anger like a fashion statement. Her arms danced wildly as she shouted and poked at her cell phone. Ruby could see the driver rolling his eyes, his expression glazing over. His dismissiveness unleashed a fury that turned her face as red as her cape. Her sharp edges reminded Ruby of her unmedicated mother and made Ruby cringe.

As she tried to erase her mother's image from her mind, the most handsome man she'd ever seen appeared at the woman's side. He moved gracefully, and stroked the woman's back, as if his tender gesture would calm her.

"Give me a minute," he said to the driver.

Hot Man looked European, with his finely tailored clothes, stylish haircut, and perfectly toned body. When he smiled, time stopped, and Ruby forgot to breathe. Something unfamiliar pulled at her insides.

The birds pecked at the windows, demanding more food.

By the time Ruby's attention had shifted back to Hot Man, a mask of worry had replaced his smile. Something fluttered inside her. She wanted him to smile again, wanted to reassure him that things have a way of working out, but she couldn't.

Her phone rang. Caller ID showed it was Donald, her boss. Why was he calling now? Without a "Hello," Donald got right to the point.

"I didn't see your numbers. Did you get the instructions I sent yesterday?"

Ruby had no time for Donald and his SalesFront nonsense. She needed to keep up with Puppet Woman, Hot Man, and the movers.

"This isn't a good time. Can I call you back in an hour?"

"I'll call you back at three," he said, hanging up before Ruby could respond.

Puppet Woman was copying license plate numbers from the black and red cars. She ripped the paper from a tiny notepad with a sharp flick of her wrist and held it out to Hot Man. He headed toward Ruby's building but stopped before entering.

"What are you waiting for?" Puppet Woman's face twisted into a scowl as she demanded an answer.

Hot Man didn't respond and instead slipped inside the building.

Ruby wanted to slap the snot right out of that woman. How dare she treat him like that! When her intercom buzzed, she jumped up and ran across the room to answer the intercom.

"Hello. Is anyone there?" It was his voice.

"Yes . . . Yes, I'm here," Ruby said, stuttering.

"Do you own either the red or the black car parked in front of the building?"

"No. No, I don't own a car." Why was she tripping over her words?

"Do you know who they belong to?"

"Sorry."

"Thanks anyway."

Before she could ask if they were moving into the building, his voice faded away.

The telephone rang. Caller ID said it was Jeffrey Marks, one of Ruby's least favorite customers. She slipped her headset on and woke her sleeping computer from its nap. What the hell did he want, and why did he have to call now just when things were getting interesting?

Keeping her tone polite, she searched her computer's files for the stats Marks wanted. During the forty-minute call, Ruby made faces and gave him the finger three times. The only thing that mattered to her was what was going on outside. New beginnings said so much, but she'd never have all the puzzle pieces if she missed something important.

The second Marks hung up, Ruby pulled her headset off and returned to the window. The moving truck was still there, but Hot Man, Puppet Woman, and the movers were gone. When she heard the clicking of the high heels followed by Puppet Woman's voice, she knew where they had gone to.

"You'd better not damage anything, or your boss is going to hear about it."

Ruby cracked her door open and watched the parade of furniture and boxes disappear into the unit next to hers. She hadn't seen her old neighbor, Jack, in weeks. When had he moved out, and how had she missed it?

Dear God, Puppet Woman was going to be her next-door neighbor. Ruby ducked back into her apartment and positioned herself at the peephole. The movers refused to speed things up, despite the woman's threats and insults. Ruby rubbed her eyes. Keeping up with other people was exhausting.

Her phone rang again. It was Donald. Was it three o'clock already? She picked up the phone and dashed back to her peephole. While he blathered on about changes they'd made to the SalesFront software, Ruby tried to keep track of what was going on next door.

She moved her hand in circles, gesturing for him to speed it up, thankful he couldn't see her. They didn't pay her enough to put in an appearance, and since she hadn't brushed her hair or changed out of her pajamas in days, she was glad she had the foresight to refuse to FaceTime with anyone ever.

Puppet Woman was prancing around on those ridiculous heels while Hot Man was letting her walk all over him. Were they together? They seemed utterly mismatched, and Ruby hoped he was a friend helping her to move. With all that was going on, how was she supposed to concentrate on Donald's SalesFront nonsense?

After the movers had finished, Hot Man followed them outside. Ruby watched as he signed the paperwork and tipped them generously to compensate for Puppet Woman's abuse.

A short while later, K-pop music invaded Ruby's apartment. It was loud, and she couldn't understand the lyrics.

"What's that noise?" Donald asked.

Damn. Ruby had forgotten she was still on the phone with him.

"My new neighbor hasn't figured out how thin the walls are."

"I've got a few more things to go over . . ."

When Ruby was finally free, she returned to the window, but Hot Man's strained, yet hushed voice was now coming from next door.

"Misa, let's turn the music down, just a little," he said.

"Why?"

Ruby pictured Puppet Woman's sharp, red talons spinning the stereo's volume knob with the force of a contestant on *The Wheel of Fortune*.

"Because it's too loud. We don't want to be bad neighbors."

"Ben, you should worry more about what I think and less about everyone else."

His real name was Ben, but he'd always be Hot Man to Ruby.

RUBY ORDERED HER DINNER, Chinese food. She'd been ordering from the Asian Palace for years and was on a first-name basis with Fang, the delivery guy. He was the only person she saw regularly.

She had eaten Chinese takeout as a child, whenever her mother wasn't in the mood to cook, which was most days. Her mother would give Ruby her credit card and tell her to order whatever she wanted from the local Chinese restaurant as long as it cost less than ten dollars. Happy Fortune's food was consistent, and consistency was something Ruby desperately needed, especially when her mother stopped taking her meds, and things went from awful to unbearable.

"The doctor said you have to take your medication, or you'll get worse," Ruby would say.

"Those pills make me a zombie," her mother said.

She had a long list of excuses for why she wouldn't take her medication. Eventually she'd wave Ruby away, saying something like, "You've been watching too much Dr. Phil."

One afternoon, when Ruby came home from school, the house was unusually quiet. She looked in every room, in every closet, frantically calling out for her mother until she found her naked and hiding in a corner of their attic. Ruby offered clothes to her and tried to coax her to get dressed. When she wouldn't respond, Ruby called her mother's psychiatrist. The psychiatrist called Social Services and a crisis intervention team was dispatched to their house.

Ruby stood on the sidelines while a social worker and two EMTs went up into the attic. When her mother threatened to kill them, the EMTs tackled and restrained her.

As they carried her mother down from the attic, she struggled violently against the tight wrappings of the transport body bag. It unnerved Ruby to watch her mother rage against everyone, like a feral animal.

"I hate you, you ungrateful bitch. You planned this," she accused.

The social worker asked Ruby if she had any family to stay with while her mother was in the hospital. Ruby didn't know where her father was. He'd left when her mother's delusions consumed her until she no longer cooked, cleaned, bathed, or slept. Ruby never understood why he hadn't taken his only child, his ten-year-old daughter, with him, or how he could leave Ruby with someone who wasn't capable of taking care of herself, much less taking care of a child.

She moved in with her grandparents that same day.

The last time Ruby had seen her mother was the night the EMTs took her away. She couldn't bring herself to visit her in the hospital. Instead, she punished herself for being a terrible daughter by confining herself to her grandparents' apartment.

Seven months after Ruby's twenty-first birthday, both grandparents died of pneumonia within weeks of each other. Ruby inherited their rent-controlled apartment, the pigeons, and her mother's agoraphobia.

Like a dutiful daughter, she didn't want her mother to feel guilty for failing at motherhood, so she called her weekly and confabulated a life for herself to reassure her mother that she hadn't passed her crazy genes on to Ruby.

Whenever her mother asked, "When are you coming to see me?" Ruby would make excuses and say her boss couldn't spare her. Her mother would drop the subject until their next phone call, and then they'd ride the same carousel.

Her mother could rant for hours, but luckily tonight her intercom buzzed and rescued her. It was Fang with her dinner.

"I have to go, Mom. Someone's at the door."

"Don't forget to tell your boss you need time off to visit your mother."

The intercom buzzed again.

"Talk to you next week."

Fang was on his way up. She'd paid for her dinner by credit card over the phone and added his tip to the charges to avoid handling cash. Cash was so dirty, so germy. Whenever Fang went on vacation or took time off, he'd let her know so she could order enough food in advance to last until he returned. Fang didn't make small talk, like other delivery people. He knocked on her door, handed her the bag with her food, and mumbled a quick thank-you. It was a relationship without demands or disappointments.

Once, a few years ago, Fang joked with her. "I always know which day of the week it is according to your order."

She blinked and then stared at him, confused, not knowing what to say.

"I mean, you keep me on track," he said.

She stared at him like an idiot.

"Okay, then. Have a nice evening."

That was the last time he made small talk.

Every night, Ruby set her table for dinner with a tablecloth, cloth napkin, and a candle. She would light a candle and put Mozart on the stereo.

She spooned bright orange carrots, crisp green celery, toasted cashews, and bite-sized pieces of chicken onto her plate. The only thing that could improve her dinner would be to have someone special to share it with. Someone like Hot Man. They'd discuss politics and current events, or recite lines from poems they'd memorized. They'd go to the ballet or opera or an off-Broadway play. Love would triumph over her agoraphobia, and she would have the life she'd always wanted. These thoughts made her aware of how empty her life was, and wondering what it would feel like to be loved.

A loud, thumping noise made her drop her chopsticks. It was the unmistakable sound of two people having sex. Ruby covered her ears and winced at the awful sound of Puppet Woman moaning, "Do me harder, baby! Harder!" How was she supposed to function with her neighbors moaning and talking dirty?

Ruby's fantasy was squashed flat. She blew out the candle and scooped her cashew chicken back into the container. Jack had always been quiet, the perfect neighbor. Maybe that wasn't such a blessing, since he had either moved out or died without her knowing. Now she had a pair of sex maniacs living next door.

They hadn't been neighbors for more than a few days when Ruby began to hate Puppet Woman for her loud sexual relationship with Hot Man. It seemed like they were doing it constantly. Didn't either of them work? Why couldn't they move their bed away from the wall? A few times, Ruby pounded on the wall to let them know she could hear them. Why couldn't they be more considerate?

They'd quiet down for a while and then be right back at it. The thumping would get faster and louder until desire overwhelmed Ruby and her hand found its way into her panties.

* * *

HOT MAN PRACTICED THE violin from noon until four every day. His music made its way into Ruby's apartment through the walls and windows. She'd pretend he was serenading her.

In the evening, she watched him leave for work. He was dressed in a black tuxedo and carried a violin case. She supposed he worked for the Metropolitan Opera House or in an orchestra on Broadway. His comings and goings were consistent. They'd make a perfect couple, except for the coming and going.

Lately, Puppet Woman was out more than she was home, sometimes staying out all night. When she returned, she and Hot Man would argue, doors would slam, and Ruby would hear someone crying. It had to be him because she couldn't imagine Puppet Woman letting anything like an emotion smudge her makeup.

The moaning and wall thumping now only happened after arguments. Was she growing tired of Hot Man? Did his routine bore her? Was she ready to move on to someone more exciting?

One afternoon, as Ruby waited behind one of her neighbors at the trash chute, Hot Man came out into the hallway. The tired expression on his face and black circles under his eyes made her want to hug him.

"Hello," she said.

He shook his head as if shaking away the cobwebs.

"I'm sorry. I don't remember your name," he said.

"It's Ruby. My apartment is next to yours."

"Is my violin playing disturbing you?"

Ruby brushed a stray hair from her face and glanced down at what she was wearing. Sweat pants and a rumpled T-shirt. Why hadn't she dressed up to take out the trash?

"Oh, no. Just the opposite. Your music is beautiful."

"Thank you, but if it's ever too loud or annoying, please let me know."

She nodded and hurried back to her apartment. What was a nice guy like Hot Man doing with that witch? Puppet Woman didn't deserve him. Why was he involved with her? It had to be the sex, although either they weren't as horny as they'd once been, or they were now doing it quietly. No. Puppet Woman would never do anything quietly. She was loud and flashy. Everything about her screamed, "Look at me!"

Ruby figured she was better suited to Hot Man than Puppet Woman was, but if she wanted him to pay attention to her, she'd have to make a few changes. First, she'd need to do something about her hair. Then she'd have to buy some new clothes. Something that enhanced her shape and hid her lumpy waistline. She could order clothes over the internet, but she'd have to leave her apartment for the haircut, which would mean leaving the building. That wasn't going to happen.

She'd almost given up her search for a nearby hair salon when she came across a business card tacked to the bulletin board in the mailroom. Sheila, of Sheila's Stylz & Profilz, was a traveling hairdresser. She was available by appointment. Travel expenses were additional. Ruby called her immediately.

Sheila answered on the third ring. Her voice had a congested, nasal quality. Ruby wondered if Sheila had a cold and hated to think about all of those germs floating around her apartment.

"I'm thinking about having my hair colored and cut," Ruby said.

"When was the last time you had your hair done?"

Ruby looked up at the ceiling and squinted as she tried to remember when she had gone to that party at Gina Di Ramo's house. Was it fourteen or fifteen years ago? Her mother had sent her to a salon with instructions for the hairdresser to make Ruby look like a princess. Ruby had walked to the salon, but on her way home the wind had picked up and she had to fight to keep her thickly lacquered hair from cracking and flying off on an aggressive gust of wind.

"I guess you could say it's been a while."

They agreed on a date and time.

Ruby's sales dwindled as she trolled the internet, day after day, for the perfect haircut. Afternoons, she would unplug her phone while

Hot Man practiced so that the ringing wouldn't disturb him. Was being attracted to a brooding musician a cliché? She didn't care.

And where was Puppet Woman? Ruby hadn't seen her in eight or nine days. She pulled the ledger out of her desk. It was exactly ten days since she'd last seen Puppet Woman leaving the building. Was she away on a business trip? Or a family emergency? Or maybe they'd broken up? Ruby's eyes sparkled and her mouth found its smile. Wouldn't it be perfect if Puppet Woman was gone for good?

Two weeks later, the downstairs buzzer rang. It was Sheila. Ruby wondered if she might still be contagious, but when Sheila rolled her suitcase into the kitchen and held out a business card instead of offering her hand, she knew she'd picked a winner.

"Do you have a picture of the cut you want?"

Sheila draped a plastic tablecloth over the kitchen table, without seeming to be bothered by the clumps of blonde hair from another client that were stuck to it. Ruby shivered and held her jaws together to keep a gasp from slipping out. When Sheila had finished unpacking her suitcase and arranging her bottles, brushes, and scissors, she took a handful of Ruby's hair and let it sift through her fingers.

"We'd better get started. I've only got two hours before my next client, and you need some serious work."

Sheila matched Ruby's brown and covered the grays. After giving her a shoulder-length bob, she dried her hair, and offered a hand-held mirror to Ruby.

Ruby looked in the mirror, tilting her head in different directions. Her hair was shorter and shiny.

"It's perfect."

Later that day, as Hot Man was leaving for work, Ruby put her coat on and went out into the hall.

"Hi," she said.

Her hands shook as she locked her apartment door. She had a plan. They'd walk down the stairs together, and when they got near the front door, Ruby would suddenly remember she'd left her wallet upstairs.

"How's it going?" he asked.

"Sales have been slow lately."

"I forgot. What do you sell?"

He didn't know because he'd never asked her before. She wondered if he noticed her new hairdo and shook her head to give him a hint.

"Ad space for the *New York Post*."

"I've wanted to work on a new piece of music, but need an honest opinion about it. Would you be willing to come over tomorrow afternoon and listen to it?"

Honesty. He valued honesty. What would he think if he knew the only reason she was walking down four flights of stairs was to spend a few minutes with him?

"I don't know much about violin music, but sure. What time?"

"Two o'clock?"

Ruby stopped walking. "Oh, darn it."

"What's wrong?"

"I forgot my wallet. I have to go back upstairs." She looked into his eyes for only a moment, but wished she could linger there for the rest of her life. "See you tomorrow at two."

Elated that her ruse paid off, Ruby ran up the four flights. Tomorrow Hot Man would play his violin just for her. Everything was working out.

At two o'clock the next day, Ruby knocked on Hot Man's door.

He welcomed her inside. "Can I get you a cup of tea or coffee?"

"No, thanks," Ruby said. She didn't want to risk spilling anything on her new clothes.

His living room was decorated in black, white, and shades of gray. There was nothing to indicating that Puppet Woman was still around.

He motioned for her to sit on the sofa as he picked up his violin.

"This piece was written in 1933 by a Hungarian composer and was originally titled 'Vége a Világnak' or 'End of the World.' It later became known as 'Gloomy Sunday,' but was also called, 'The Hungarian Suicide Song,' because an urban legend claimed that many people had committed suicide while listening to it. It was banned from the radio in Hungary, England, and several other countries."

Ruby's smile disappeared.

"Why do you want to play it?"

"There's something incredibly beautiful and haunting about this piece. I can't get it out of my mind."

When he rested the violin against his chin and his bow made contact with the strings, Ruby stopped breathing. The suffering of every broken-hearted lover suddenly filled the room. Each tortured note twisted his pain into something she couldn't bear to witness. She felt as if she was suffocating under the weight of those who had chosen to kill themselves rather than live without love.

When he had finished, Ruby wiped away her tears and breathed again.

"It's beautiful. I see what you mean."

From then on, Hot Man added "Gloomy Sunday" to his practice repertoire, some days playing it over and over, until Ruby felt she needed to check on him.

"Come in and pardon the mess," he said, pointing to the sheet music scattered on the floor and the half-eaten takeout containers on the coffee table.

The buttons on his shirt were misaligned, and his hair was uncombed. He also looked thinner and paler than the last time she had seen him up close. Her mouth was dry, and she couldn't stop rubbing her sweaty hands together as she worked up the courage to ask him if he was suicidal or mourning Puppet Woman's absence.

"I'm not sure how to say this. It's about that piece of music."

"The 'Gloomy Sunday' piece?"

"Yes." Ruby had to know if he was okay. She continued, "What was your girlfriend's name?"

"You mean Misa?"

She nodded. "What happened to her?"

She couldn't stop her hands from shaking as she told him she worried he might be depressed or suicidal. His circumstances seemed to fit with the urban legend, and she didn't want anything to happen to him.

"Misa is a drug I can't get out of my system. The music helps me to let go." Hot Man stood up. "I'm sorry. Sometimes I get caught up in it."

Ruby sighed. Now she'd never be able to tell him she was in love with him. And what kind of name was Misa? Ruby loved Hot Man. Hot Man loved Puppet Woman. And Puppet Woman loved herself. No one was destined to be happy.

"I feel badly for making you worry. Let me make it up to you," he said as he ran his hands over his face. "Antonio Viadelmonte, the young tenor from Naples, is premiering at the Met next month in *Pagliacci*. Would you be my guest? I'll be working, but I could meet you for a drink or dinner after the concert."

"I . . . I couldn't. It's too much." Ruby stood up. How could she go to an opera at the Met when she couldn't even leave the building?

Hot Man pressed the ticket into her hand. "Please?"

The heat from his touch burned through her. She needed to get back to the safety of her apartment.

"I'd love to," she said.

As she rushed away, she wondered where those words had come from. Had she actually said them aloud? She locked the door behind her and plopped down onto her sofa, the still-warm ticket in her hand. Puppet Woman was his drug. But Puppet Woman was gone, and Ruby was here. Was it possible he might fall in love with her? Or was he Ruby's drug?

She scraped the polish off her fingernails while she paced back and forth. If she wanted to have a life, she'd have to step out of her comfort zone. Isn't that what her last therapist had told her?

Charlie, Hairy Harry, and Grace marched along the ledge, mirroring Ruby's movements. Pip-Squeak was probably snoozing somewhere off to the side.

"Focus, Ruby, focus."

Until now, Ruby had spent her entire adult life as a bystander, as a voyeur and prisoner, watching the world from her apartment, never reaching out or allowing people inside. Was she destined to spend the rest of her life alone, without knowing what it would feel like to be held by a man? She wanted this desperately, but didn't know if she could get herself out into the world in four short weeks. If she wanted to go to this concert, she'd have to train like an Olympic athlete.

She'd map out a route to the Met, break her mission into small steps, and chart her progress. She'd order one of those fancy fitness trackers to keep track of her steps, and a book on training strategies for athletes.

Two days later, her fitness tracker and book arrived. She ignored her customers' phone calls and instead read about training strategies. The author said you had to visualize yourself at the finish line, the winner of the race. If you could see yourself there, you could get yourself there. She closed her eyes and visualized their date.

It took three days and countless tries for Ruby to make it past the mailroom and into the lobby. Gradually, she made it to the same spot but was now no longer hyperventilating as people walked past her. A few people were looking at their phones instead of where they were going and bumped into her. She hissed at them.

She practiced her steps while he practiced his violin. It was ironic how she had spent her time behind a pane of glass, looking out at people, while he spent most of his time looking inward to find the music inside him.

Four more days had passed and Ruby still hadn't stepped outside. The concert was three weeks away, and she literally had a lot of ground to cover before she'd be ready. Yet self-doubt growled at her, making her feel like a fraud, chiding her to tell him the truth. It wasn't fair to lead him on. What could she offer to someone as talented and handsome as Hot Man?

The training manual said not to give up, no matter how much or how little progress she was making. It was still progress. She squelched the saboteur inside her head and continued. As she opened the door and stepped one foot over the threshold, a gust of wind slammed the door shut on her ankle. She yelped in pain as she opened the door and freed her foot. Her stockings were ruined and there was a bloody gash across her instep.

Her injured foot had become so swollen it wouldn't fit into her shoes. Going anywhere during her second week of training was now out of the question. From the comfort of her sofa, she imagined herself inside a yellow checkered cab, telling the driver to take her to the Met. She could still make it, she told herself, and visualization was as important as actually going outside.

Somewhere between weeks two and three, whenever Ruby was getting ready to leave her apartment, the phone would ring. Sometimes it was her boss, other times it was a customer, but most often it was her mother. The doctors were trying her on a new medication, and she rambled on, rarely pausing long enough for Ruby to get a word in. When she tried ending her mother's calls, her mother would accuse her of not caring. How could she be so cruel? Guilt kept her on the phone, derailing her training, while her mother's raspy voice taunted her.

"You'll never make it. No one wants you. You're pathetic."

That last remark hurt the most. The needy child inside of Ruby couldn't bring herself to ignore her mother's choice of words that scraped away the crumbs of Ruby's self-esteem. She'd been a fool for thinking she had ever had a chance.

Days before the concert, Ruby teetered between giving up and risking it all. More than anything, she wanted to go to that concert and out to dinner with Ben, but her mother's voice kept telling her she was a nobody. Whatever courage she had knitted together, her mother worked to unravel.

Then there was the call from Donald that told her she was in serious trouble.

"Houston, we have a problem," he said.

"What? What's going on?"

"Your sales are down, and two of your customers complained to corporate that you haven't followed through on their orders. We need to have a meeting."

"Donald, I haven't left my apartment in years. A meeting is out of the question. Hang on while I pull up my spreadsheets."

Ruby opened her monthly sales document. Damn it! Donald was right. Her sales had slipped.

"Sorry," she said. "I'll hammer this out right away. You'll never know there was an issue."

After hanging up, she checked on her pigeons. Three were huddled together, but Pip-Squeak was off by herself again. This was the second or third time she had noticed Pip-Squeak isolating from the others.

She opened the window and said, "Take it from me, isolating can make you crazy."

Pip-Squeak looked up and then tucked her head into her wing.

Hot Man had finished practicing for the day. He still played "Gloomy Sunday" occasionally, but only once or twice before moving on. She watched him leave for work. Everything looked so easy for him.

An hour later, Ruby heard noises coming from next door. Was Hot Man back already? Was he sick? She knocked on his door and gasped aloud when Puppet Woman answered.

Ruby stammered. "I saw Ben leave for work, and then I heard noises. I wanted to make sure he was okay."

"How neighborly of you to check on him."

Puppet Woman's condescending expression made Ruby shudder.

"We were taking a break. You know, absence makes the heart grow fonder and all that." Puppet Woman stared down at Ruby. "Break's over."

"Right. Well, welcome back." Ruby forced herself to smile as she backed herself into her apartment and shut the door. Why had Hot Man been so friendly and why hadn't he mentioned Puppet Woman's return? What was she supposed to do now?

She clenched both her fists and teeth as she paced back and forth. She'd made some progress and was almost ready for their date. Almost. But the more she thought about Puppet Woman's return, the angrier she became. Why couldn't that witch stay away? Couldn't he see how that woman was like a cat that toys with a mouse before killing it? Aside from her looks, what did she have that Ruby didn't?

Everything. She had Hot Man.

The morning of the concert, Hot Man knocked on Ruby's door. She checked her teeth in the mirror and fluffed her hair.

"What's up?" she said.

With his hands in his pockets, he avoided making eye contact and instead looked at the floor.

"I feel like a jerk for asking, but I'm in a bind. Misa insisted I get her into Viadelmonte's premier. She had a fit when I told her I'd given my guest ticket away and threatened to leave if I didn't get it back."

Ruby's mouth gaped when she realized Puppet Woman had eliminated her from the competition, and all it had taken was a single hissy fit. She handed Hot Man the ticket and mumbled something about a cold coming on and how it would be best if she stayed home, anyway.

"A Viadelmonte concert is probably more Misa's kind of thing than mine," she said. "See you around."

Ruby threw herself onto her bed and cried. Hot Man had just committed the ultimate betrayal.

Later that afternoon, he left for the Met at his usual time. After crossing the street, he looked up toward Ruby's window, waved to her, and mouthed the words "Thank you."

Ruby's hand pressed against the windowpane, poised to catch his kiss, but there was no kiss to be had. Her hand remained there long after he'd turned and walked away. She'd never suffered a broken heart before and didn't know what to do with this awful hurt. Her mother was right. Ruby was a nobody and didn't deserve to be loved. She threw herself onto her sofa and stifled her groans with an expensive accent pillow. This was the worst thing she'd ever felt. Once Puppet Woman left the building, Ruby released her grief as if she were a wailing widow.

Hairy Harry, Grace, and Charlie were at the window, looked for the source of the strange noise. They pounded against the glass, like woodpeckers on a mission, until they got her attention.

"I can take a hint," she said, wiping her tears away. She opened a window and petted them. They were soft and nuzzled her hand with their heads. They weren't much of a family, but she loved them and supposed she should be grateful for their love.

The next day, Ruby woke up with puffy eyes and splotchy skin. She couldn't believe she had slept until twelve-thirty and was thankful she didn't have to be anywhere. Her newspaper was waiting for her outside her apartment door. She scooped it up and brewed a pot of coffee. The review of Viadelmonte's concert took up nearly half a page in the entertainment section. It had been a grand premiere. Ruby would have had an even grander premiere if she had gone to the Met. But that was old news now. Her fantasy had been trampled by Puppet Woman's return.

She opened her windows to feed the pigeons. Grace, Hairy Harry, and Charlie woke up and pecked at the birdseed. She couldn't see Pip-Squeak, so she opened the window wider and stuck her head outside. Pip-Squeak was huddled in the far corner of the ledge and wasn't moving. Ruby called out to her, but she didn't respond. Nudging the other birds off to the side, Ruby leaned out as far as she could, but still couldn't reach her.

Without thinking, Ruby grabbed a small tote bag and reminded herself not to look down while she climbed out onto the ledge and crept forward on her knees.

A crowd gathered on the street below. Someone yelled, "Jump, lady, jump! Let's see if you can fly."

Ruby wanted to shake her fist at the guy taunting her, but needed to focus. If her eyes wandered, she would lose both her courage and her balance. Instead, she stared at Pip-Squeak and ignored everything and everyone else.

It hadn't occurred to her she was outside until the sun's warmth on her face and the gentle breeze blowing her hair into her eyes reminded her of her childhood when she used to play outside in the backyard. She and her friends would run and jump and twirl about until they fell over from dizziness or exhaustion. She used to have friends. Tears slipped down her cheeks. Ruby was actually outside! And it felt amazing! She allowed herself to linger in her victory until reality interrupted her moment.

Oh, hell. How was she going to get back inside?

Crawling backward on a narrow ledge while holding a bag seemed impossible. Was this supposed to be some sort of metaphor for her life? Was her big reward for breaking free of her partially self-imposed prison a fall to her death?

Sirens blared in the distance. Police walkie-talkies clicked on and off, turning voices into static as the crowd continued to grow.

She was relieved when the police positioned a jump cushion below her. She wasn't suicidal, but maybe she should be. Hot Man and Puppet Woman were on again, and any possibility of a relationship between Ruby and Hot Man was gone. Hurt scraped at her heart until she scolded herself for thinking about her love life, when she should be thinking about Pip-Squeak.

She stretched her arm and hand as far as it would go, yet she was still inches from where Pip-Squeak lay. As if sensing Ruby needed her help, Pip-Squeak looked at Ruby and then dragged her body along the rough ledge until she collapsed in Ruby's sweaty palm.

With the tote bag dangling from the crook of her elbow, Ruby inched her way backward, her body pressing against the building as her foot searched for the window's opening. She'd have to slide one leg at a time into the opening while keeping her upper body from swaying. If she was going to fall, she wanted to fall into her apartment, so the jerk taunting her wouldn't have the last laugh.

At the first note of "Gloomy Sunday," Ruby froze. Its tragic melody gutted her. How could Hot Man be so oblivious, as if nothing was wrong? If she fell to her death, like the unrequited lovers who had propelled themselves off bridges and rooftops, would her pain end? Or would her suffering be even greater if she survived? Her muscles tensed, and her throat ached from the lifetime of feelings rushing out of her. Each note pushed her deeper and deeper under water, blocking out the noise from the crowd below. Ruby squeezed her eyes shut. Maybe she was better off dead. The only thing she knew for sure was that she couldn't go back to her solitary confinement.

And then she entertained a truly wicked thought. She imagined herself falling and landing on Puppet Woman. Puppet Woman's arms would be burdened with expensive shopping bags, and since she'd never given Ruby a second thought, she'd never see her coming. By the time Ruby landed on her, she'd be dead, like the wicked witch in *The Wizard of Oz*. She wouldn't cushion Ruby's landing, but it would be à propos. Ruby's expression brightened.

"What's taking so long? Jump, lady! Get it over with!"

Why was this guy egging her on? Was she some kind of freak show? Did her life mean nothing?

A police officer with a bullhorn spoke to her.

"Okay, lady, let's not do anything crazy now. It's not worth it. Can you tell me your name?"

Ruby ignored the cop's psycho talk. Instead, she listened as Ben finished playing the last note of "Gloomy Sunday." Then she opened her eyes.

The cop shouted, "Lady, go back inside."

But Ruby didn't want to go back inside. She didn't want to be alone or lonely anymore. The more the cop and heckler demanded of her, the more she wanted to be in charge of her own destiny. For once, she refused to listen to anyone telling her who she was or what she could do. A slow surge of power coursed through her veins, making her feel as if she could do anything.

She was outside, and she hadn't panicked. Her world was in perfect focus, and she breathed easily for the first time in her life. The hurt, fear, and pain that had imprisoned her for years had been weakened. Ruby saved Pip-Squeak, and now she would save herself because the world was waiting for her.

Confession of a Female Bodybuilder

Mia Cara Kinsella

If I spoke my mind for a day
I would tell everyone
That being a girl
With muscle
Is okay.

"You're bulking?"
Shock ripples their face
Not the answer expected when invading my space
To comment on my body
Apparently it's sooo out of place

How could any female ever want to take up more space?
Why would a girl be here not to shrink?
To do cardio until her feet snap at the ankle
Till she is skin and bones and a bloody cankle?

Why would a girl want to be strong?
To stand in a weight room surrounded by men all day long?
Three hours a day
Six days a week

What would a girl gain from such a masculine environment?
Women are supposed to be meek and avoid gluten into
    retirement.

"Aren't you scared?"
"I would never do that"
"You are going to get bulky from lifting so heavy"
"Don't hurt yourself darling, really that's plenty"
"You're just a little girl you don't need that much protein"
"You want to be looked at that's why you're here"
"Take up yoga and running so you can shrink and disappear"

"Sorry girl I don't wanna lift with you
I respect the dedication but I would never wanna look like you
    do"
As if picking up a dumbbell will immediately make them huge.

What a horrifying thought to be larger
To be muscular like a man
Since femininity is "gender specific"
She can't move weights but he can

I am suddenly aware of my shoulders and quads
Maybe they're not supposed to stick out
Maybe I should hop on the treadmill
Forget my goals
My dreams
My confidence
The power I feel when I hit a new PR
Maybe my traps are a trap
Maybe I should cut my calories and take a lap
Maybe I shouldn't hit upper body,
They warned it would make me square,

Maybe I should stop trying
Maybe I would be better small

Your body's supposed to be constantly lean
We want you as skinny as possible
With a huge ass
And massive tits
Don't hit chest
You'll lose what little boobs you have—

But hey! maybe then I won't be noticed
When I walk into the weight room
Or someone won't help but approach me
To dissect my body

They don't seem to realize that they're being mean
They ask when my cut is going to begin
They say they hope that it's soon.

He says not to gain too much more muscle
Be careful
When did being impressed by my lifts become warnings of
   losing my femininity,
As if it is something physically attached to me?
I almost want to conform just to quiet the stupidity

Sometimes I feel like a zoo animal,
Instead of me doing something I love.
The gym can be a community
A kind place of support
But the unsolicited comments
And warnings
Make me question myself in my sport

They're missing the point
They don't understand
To be strong
And take up space
Is not a disgrace
"Why would she want that?"
Why wouldn't she?

If I spoke my mind for a day
I would tell society
That being a girl
With muscle
Is okay.

After Hiker Midnight

Kayla Agnir

HIKER MIDNIGHT.

The term may be alien if you're not a seasoned, long-distance hiker, along with *blue blazing, yellow blazing,* and the ever-imprudent *pink blazing.* There are *PUDs, LASHers, widow makers, zeros,* and *neros.* The *purists* often look down on *slack packing,* and if there's a long stretch without reliable water, like my eighteen-mile section in *Rocksylvania* or in New York where every water source seemed to be farmland runoff, you had better *camel up* or else pray for a *trail angel.* Those who set out to hike the 2,000+ miles of the Appalachian Trail in one go are destined to make it to their endpoint with a whole host of hiker vernacular.

Hiker Midnight. The word combination holds an air of mystery and intrigue befitting the small percentage of people willing to traverse fourteen consecutive states on foot. Traveling through the woods, hikers are hidden from the outside world, existing as slivers of forms striding between dense trees, while midnight carries its own connotation of being dark and witchy—catering to the unknown. Unfortunately, the definition hardly lives up to the image conjured.

9:00 p.m.?!

What deception! There's something called "Hiker Midnight" and it equates to "bedtime on a school night"? I was determined to push past my limits, and hellbent on having an adventure teeming with excitement and uncertainty. I was a solo female hiker yearning to catch a glimpse of things that go bump in the night in hopes of receiving an invitation to become one. I wanted the damn hiker *witching hour*!

Hiker Midnight: the time most hikers are tucked into their sleeping bags. They have long since set up their tents and hammocks, inflated their sleeping pads, fetched tomorrow's water, and cooked and eaten dinner—all by a regimented 5:00 p.m. It was not unusual to pass by a shelter when the sun was still high overhead and see hikers in their tents, thumbing through guidebooks to plan tomorrow's water stops and lunch breaks. I hated the routine nature of it, no pun intended.

I initially started night hiking by accident. Truthfully, it was because I have a penchant for lazy mornings, along with a love affair with the inside of my eyelids. I like a slow start. At some point, I stopped trying to kid myself with the "out of camp by 7 and in bed by 5" mentality. I couldn't even do that with societal constructs in place, never mind while living in the woods for months on one of the oldest thru-hiking trails in the United States. Out there, it seemed like everything about the trail—its ancient, dense forest with knobby trees, glacial deposits, and mossy floors—begged me to take my time and grow older where I lay. So, I would leave camp around 11 a.m., a time when other hikers were generally enjoying the first break for food, and continued hiking until I ended at, or came close to, my intended destination of the day—steady like the tortoise. This brought me to crossing the threshold of Hiker Midnight.

At some point, I realized that keeping these odd hours wouldn't allow me to make the miles I needed *and* get under the covers before the lights went out. But a headlamp is a beautiful invention. With a click of a button, I could emblazon my path (at least for up to 100 or so meters in the direction of my gaze). Armed with my artificial daylight as dusk faded to night, I began to experience the trail with altered senses.

The first things I noticed were the nearly invisible. The ones only seen as a reflection of light. Distinctly shaped eyes watching me from within the woods—the narrowly spaced eyes of deer and big round eyes of black bears. Insects' armored bodies and silky spider webs. Mica and other minerals that glint and sparkle like a sky full of stars. Then, as I started to adjust to the darkness, I became aware of the deafening sounds all around. Every creaking limb, the moan of the wind, the chatter of foxes, and the powerful symphony of bugs, frogs, and thousands of other nameless creatures. Hiking longer into the night makes way for rare gifts not often granted during the day. I stopped for a large rattlesnake that cruised across the trail while I waited for it like it was a passing train. It did not acknowledge me, and maybe did not even sense me. The night became alive and provided its own illumination in the form of a full moon, or a burning field of fireflies—sights that only exist in contrast to darkness.

I encountered a sleeping fawn, no larger than a housecat, left by its mother in a safe place by the edge of the trail, close to where she knew humans were more plentiful, and where predators would keep their distance. It didn't stir, as were the mother's instructions, and I was able to sit and watch its auburn fur with small, white spots move up and down with every breath. Another time, my brow became a perch for an enormous cecropia moth with a six-inch wingspan, drawn in by the allure of my small, but powerful, beacon. I was simultaneously part of the landscape and an observer. I climbed down steep mountain staircases with massive steps that could have been part of a giant's castle. I paused on leaf-covered ground by strange rock formations and stared at the spaces between the trees, hesitantly hoping to steal a glimpse of the witch, U'tlun'ta. I walked across vast rock ridges on twinkling sand and imagined I was a lone astronaut on the surface of the moon.

After a particularly long night that had transformed back into morning (since time had moved with me, step-in-step), I came across a novelty—a four-walled shelter with a real door. There were hikers in various stages of getting ready, some scraping the last bits of breakfast from their cups, and others drinking their *graywater*. A few more appeared in the doorway and wore puzzled looks as I said hello and made my way inside. I pulled out my sleeping bag and proceeded to blow up my pad. They stared as I kicked off my trail runners and climbed into my newly made bed. Then, one of them finally asked what the others were thinking.

"What shelter did you come from this morning?"

"Oh me?" I responded. "I just finished for the night."

They exchanged looks, trying to make sense of the small woman in front of them, their gears turning over this break with convention—a page of some rulebook being ripped to shreds. I removed my priceless headlamp, stashed it in my pack, and settled into my sleeping bag with the hood positioned over my face to block out the incoming morning rays. Feeling no urgency, no need to race the sun whether it came or went, I stretched fully against the walls of my cocoon, letting my muscles contract and then relax, heavy with the weight of every step traveled. I could feel their eyes on me; the silence from their unasked questions made the air feel stagnant, like we were all frozen for the moment, both parties on the verge of speaking. I thought of how to explain that I felt compelled to walk in the dark, to find the words to describe how the environment transformed—and me with it—and how rounding each bend revealed new parts of an uncharted world. This time, the questions never came, and I held my peace. With my eyes shut and sense of hearing still heightened, I pictured the group, now in motion, in vivid detail—buckles clipping, zipper teeth pulling together, laces tying with double and triple knots—as they finished gathering the contents of their individual journeys. They hoisted their packs, with weight strategically balanced, walked through the door, and closed it behind them. I turned my focus inward. I let the hypnagogic waves wash over me as I drifted to sleep. My body lay still with limbs folded—waiting to emerge.

The Wise-Ass Doesn't Fall Far from the Tree

Don Carter

My father was a reserved man but that didn't affect
me. In my faith I am considered a wise-ass because my
mother was a wise-ass.

To meet my mother was to be instantly won over by her oversized
personality and generous sense of humor. She was a product of the
great state of Indiana, and in the parlance of her Hoosier upbringing,
my mother Tessie was *a hoot*. She waged war on the safe, the
conventional, and the reserved. Laughter was her ammunition and she
always left the chamber empty.

Children were particularly drawn to my mother, as they found
her to be colorful, entertaining, and prone to mischief. They invariably
looked upon her with a wide-eyed expression of shock, awe, and
adoration. At our community picnics, my mother was the one
surrounded by the neighborhood kids. She didn't know a single chord
but you'd find her ferociously strumming a poorly tuned guitar and
belting out rockabilly anthems like "Does Your Chewing Gum Lose Its
Flavor on the Bedpost Overnight." More often than not she forgot the
words, but she would make up a fresh, funnier verse right on the spot.
And when she ran out of words, she'd create sounds. When we thought
it couldn't get any funnier, she would start yodeling. That's right—

yodeling, because everyone knows the cornfields of Indiana are so much like the Swiss Alps.

In addition to her role as entertainer, Mom was the family doctor and chief fort builder. Her inexhaustible humor was the balm for our bee stings, measles, and broken bones, but she could also build a fortress out of couch cushions and laundry still warm from the dryer (which she preferred over folding). In her role as head cheerleader, she taught us that no goal was unattainable. Give us a vacant field and a shovel and we'd dig an underground fortress a Kentucky coal miner would envy. Give us a pile of discarded plumbing pipes and a lawnmower from the trash heap and we'd build a motorized contraption capable of transporting us to faraway neighborhoods, or more often, to nearby hospitals. Give us a net, a jar, and a tub and we'd build a zoo with creatures both fuzzy and slimy. It was all we could do to keep the family pets from eating one another.

When I was seven years old our floorboard heating ducts became home to a dozen tiny reptiles after my brother Jeff dropped a glass jar filled with baby snakes that we had captured in the nearby woods. Like fireworks bursting from a Fourth of July rocket, the snakes slithered in every direction and disappeared into the ductwork before we could recapture them. Another parent might have been mortified, but my mother swept up the broken glass and sent us outside with a new jar.

One brisk morning Mom thought the family gerbils needed fresh air so she placed their cage near the window. When Jeff and I came home from school on a lunch break, we discovered the gerbils had died from the draft. Jeff was heartbroken when he returned to school that afternoon, but when one of his classmates filled him with false hope he ran home hollering, "They're not dead! They're hibernating!"

Mom leapt into action like an ER trauma nurse. We watched in wonder as she turned the oven to its lowest temperature, spread the gerbils on a baking sheet and slid them in. She kept the door open so she could slide the tray out, perform CPR on their tiny chests, and then slide the tray back into the oven.

That was the mystical world my mother created. We grew up in an Adventureland where anything was possible and maybe, just maybe, gerbils could be brought back to life. If a bat flew into our living room, it became a pet. When a turtle wandered into our backyard, our only bathtub became its new home. It turned out that Mom, the super woman we believed capable of miracles, could not raise the dead, but the idea that she tried made the loss more bearable.

MOM HAD A VOCABULARY that was all her own and often made up words to suit her audience. Her favorite word was "shit," but when we had company, she cleaned it up by saying "shitáye," which she claimed was French and therefore much classier. She called my sisters "little shits." They were twins so they weren't "big shit" and "little shit." They were both "little shits." My older brother Doug was the "big shit." Apparently, my family was full of shit.

Not only did Mom make up words, she rearranged common expressions, unwittingly creating hilarious juxtapositions. Ask her about her trip to the salon and she would gush, "Oh, they treated me like the Queen of Elizabeth." (This is particularly amusing to anyone familiar with the industrial wasteland that is Elizabeth, New Jersey.)

Perhaps Mom's greatest perversion of the English language was the way she confused vowels to great, but unintended, comedic effect. Before I brought Caroline home to meet my parents, I told my mother how much my future wife loved her Volvo. When they were introduced, my mother made a point of asking Caroline about her car. My unsuspecting fiancée was understandably caught off guard when Mom kicked off the dinner table conversation with, "So, dear, tell me about your Vulva."

Caroline was busy wiping up the drink she'd spit all over the table, so I stepped in and said, "Well, Mom, I've put a lot of miles on it, but it still gets me where I want to go."

Mom liked to make a grand entrance, and the night she met Caroline's extended family illustrates the shock and awe that tended to follow her into a room. My niece Elysia was newly married when she nervously agreed to host Thanksgiving dinner in her new home. In addition to Elysia's immediate family, the guest list included her new in-laws from California and my mother. Mom marched into the crowded kitchen and before any introductions could be made, she declared, "I can't wear this bra another minute!"

As the astonished guests watched, Mom's arms disappeared inside her blouse, a short struggle ensued, and like Houdini escaping a strait jacket, her arms burst out of the sleeves with bra in hand.

"Ahh, that's better." She then turned to Elysia's dumbstruck mother-in-law, extended her empty hand, and said, "Hi, I'm Tessie. Nice to meet you." After the bra incident (as it came to be known), my mother settled in for some serious misbehaving.

When my son Christian was in high school, we held a concert in our backyard for his rock 'n' roll band. My mother, short, round, and eighty-something, hobbled on stage between sets and grabbed the microphone. I felt a familiar tingle of unease and thought, "Oh my God. What's she up to now?"

Like some Borscht Belt comedian from a bygone era, she told a few jokes and then turned to her grandson and said, "I love you, honey. This is for you."

She started to yodel and I found myself magically transported back to those long-ago community picnics. The familiar sensation of shock and awe washed over me, but it was shock and awe with a smile. It felt warm and familiar, like the toasty laundry my mother packed into the couch cushion fortresses she built on snowy days. The crowd rose from their lawn chairs in unison, the adults whooping and whistling, the children wide-eyed and open-mouthed. The thunderous applause that followed interrupted my reverie and I turned back to the stage to see Mom hold her arm out with authority, pause for effect, and then drop the mic.

* * *

MY MOTHER MAY HAVE liked a grand entrance but she *loved* a grand exit, and she did her best to *leave 'em laughing*. Mom was a commanding force of nature, a personality so immense that nothing less than a worldwide pandemic could stop her. In March of 2020 Mom made her final grand entrance into a hospital coronavirus ward.

Laughter was hard to come by as wailing sirens announced the relentless arrival of fear and hopelessness at emergency room doors. Into this despair, bleary-eyed EMTs wheeled my ninety-year-old mother . . . alone . . . the comforting presence of her children forbidden. Despite the heart-wrenching circumstances, I wasn't surprised when the nurse on duty called to say, "Your mom is amazing!" In a voice cracking with emotion, she continued, "She has every nurse in the ward laughing out loud!"

I imagined the scene:

Mom rolls into the hospital on a gurney, an oxygen mask covering her mouth and a nurse urgently checking her vital signs.

"Are you comfortable?" shouts the nurse over the din of the corridor. "Can I get you anything?"

Mom motions for the nurse to come near and weakly pulls the mask from her face.

"Yes, dear, I'll have an extra dry martini with a twist."

As Mom lay in a deathbed her family was prohibited from visiting, bewildered nurses, overworked social workers, and one particularly curious chaplain became the pipeline that funneled information to me and my terrified siblings.

Chaplain Mary introduced herself and said, "You must tell me about your mother."

I resisted her attempts to draw me into this conversation but I relented when she added, "The nursing staff, the administrators, even the maintenance crew wants to know about the woman who made them laugh when she arrived,"

In time I found myself sharing some of the family lore that comes from a lifetime spent with a misbehaving mother. At first,

Chaplain Mary seemed weary and shaken from the carnage of the pandemic, but as I talked on about my mother her demeanor brightened and she surprised me with spontaneous fits of laughter. The sound seemed out of place, but soon its magic washed over both of us and we were joined in cathartic relief.

The cause and effect of shared laughter has magnetic appeal, drawing people together in spite of, or sometimes because of, mutual suffering. But there's an unpredictable balance between humor and grief. Many people believe them to be mutually exclusive, that somehow tears are nobler than laughter and the presence of comedy in the face of suffering is inappropriate. Other people, people like my mother, believe them to be codependent. To Mom, laughter offered deliverance, a life raft in an inhospitable sea. Where we as individuals draw the line between what is funny and what is not, is simply a matter of degree. Humor does not divide us; it is what connects us in our shared humanity. In fact, nine out of ten orthopedists agree that it is the funny bone that separates us from the animals.

Of all the things I learned during the pandemic, the saddest and most telling lesson was that 2020 was an inconvenient time to die. Family members could not get on an airplane to attend services, as it was far too dangerous and irresponsible. Conventional outlets for mourning—church services, funerals, and wakes—were banned for groups of ten or more. Even small services were suspended as funeral homes overflowed and tractor trailers were transformed into makeshift morgues.

For centuries cultures have developed traditions designed to help people cope with grief and hasten the mourning process. Those of us left behind felt deprived and unsure as we struggled to independently process the pain of loss. There was little we could do except cry into our facemasks and wait for the day we might shed our plastic gloves and join hands in celebration of a life filled with laughter, love, and song. It was these qualities that drew people to my mother; that, plus she made a delicious bourbon old-fashioned.

I always knew my mother's sense of humor insulated her from the boring and the conventional, but what I didn't know, what it took her death to reveal, was that she used laughter to shield others from her pain. As I revisited Mom's life it dawned on me that her humor, like the salve for my bee stings, was the balm that would continue to comfort me in the tough days and months to come. In my conversations with Chaplain Mary, I recognized my mother's gift. Her memory would survive through the stories we tell, but it was the humor she embedded in the psyche of her children that would live on, perhaps for generations to come.

During my last conversation with Chaplain Mary, she said, "Your mother brought light into the darkness. Her laughter and bravery gave hope to a weary and frightened emergency room staff." We talked on for a few minutes longer, neither of us wanting to let go of the comfort found in shared loss. For several days we had been joined in pain and laughter and I knew that once we hung up Chaplain Mary would fade into a faceless memory.

"The world may have gone mad, Donald, but it's nice to see you've kept your sense of humor. You're a hoot and I can see the acorn didn't fall far from the tree."

A smile crossed my face. "In my family we say, the wise-ass didn't fall far from the tree."

Unlearning Their Forced Desire for Me to Become Someone I'm Not

Aurora Bones

Homeless Larry tells me a fun fact—*Did you know?*
I could be (—and I quote—) "actually very pretty"
if I dyed my hair blonde.
(—"or at least brown"—he adds as a belated compromise).
He says this like it's a huge secret he's letting me in on,
like he's offering a tip from an expert position (himself)
to me, a poor girl who just can't figure it out.

He stares at me like an artist with a vision,
the way in those teen movies from the '90s
they take off the ugly girl's glasses
& straighten her hair,
to reveal that—*gasp!*—there was a hot girl lurking beneath all
along.

Larry looks at me like he can see the hot girl underneath the
mess,
like he's just waiting for the goddess of his pornos
to emerge from this wreckage of my DIY neon-green pixie cut.

When I don't say anything, Homeless Larry spits in my hair,
then asks me for a dollar.

*

Flash back to another Larry I once knew:
one of the popular boys in high school who wrote me a note
saying he would (—and I do quote—):
"*consider* dating me if I would stop wearing so much black, &
if I would *please* for Christ's sake *QUIT KISSING GIRLS*."

I write back: *Dear Sir:*
I can see you are rather jealous
that certain lasses at our institution
would prefer to kiss my own plump & exfoliated lips
instead of your own thin, chapped, and scraggly ones.

To be clear:
there is no number high enough
to list all the things you would need to change about yourself
before I would ever consider dating YOU.

His shock. The Unthinkable. I am supposed to want
nothing more than his attention.
I am supposed to
be willing to change
anything
about myself to get it.

*

I do not want to grow my hair out;
I do not want to dye it blonde.
I do not want to quit kissing girls.
Kissing girls happens to be
one of my favorite activities.

What I would like would be to keep kissing girls,
& also to be left the fuck alone about it.

*

So the Larrys of the world don't like you
won't love you

maybe he would / maybe he could

if you lost 35 lbs
if you practiced pilates every morning with religious fervor,
if you started skipping dinner.
If you would quit
wearing so much bright makeup,

and especially
you would certainly need to quit
trying to kiss girls in the shower
or on those cross-country meets
in Chicago.

*

I haven't seen Homeless Larry since the meth house he was
    sleeping behind
blew up.
I'm sure that he's alright though:
between his flicking switchblade and his rabid smile,
only a fool or a madman would mess with Homeless Larry.

I imagine sometimes how it must feel
to move through this world feeling able
to protect yourself.
That must be the most free feeling of all.

One day I would like to walk through dark alleys unafraid.
One day I would like to be someone who could look someone in
    the eyes and say:
"don't talk to me that way,
don't touch me like that."

*

There is so much outside of me that I cannot change.
And yet. There is also so much that I can.

I begin by staring into a mirror,
practice saying assertive phrases like
"Stop!" and "No!" as if my voice were a weapon—
to command these words with such force
the words themselves will halt a man
mid-gesture.

The Crows at Countryside

Heather Murray

THE CANVAS GROCERY BAG WAS FILLED WITH PRODUCE: LEAFY GREENS, strawberries, mangos, grapes, and some cut stems of fresh flowers. I stared into the bag, enchanted by the colors. In the city, this would have cost a fortune. But out here, we could buy a bag every week and not worry about the cost.

In a past life, there was traffic. There were sirens and car horns and LED billboards. I had a job at one time, you know. I had health benefits. I was an assistant at our family business. Independence had been sweet and brief for me before the insanity set in.

I glanced up to see the back kitchen door swinging as Janie sauntered in from the garden. She dropped her dark sunglasses down her nose and looked at the grocery bag.

"Anything good?" Janie's onyx-colored hair was always pulled up in a bun or ponytail that was so tight, it might have been doing the job of a mediocre facelift. As always, she stank of hay.

"I picked up stuff for the week," I said. "We're having chili tonight. Have you been riding?"

"Just put him back in the stables." Janie moved across the kitchen and poured some water from the sink. "When do you think they'll let me go to the store?"

"Maybe when you stop trying to escape with Travis."

Travis was the tall, dark, and handsome horse that Janie took out of the stables every so often to ride on the trails.

"That was months ago." Janie still had her sunglasses on. "I'll be dead before they give me the permissions that you have."

I snorted in response.

I'd been there a long time, so they trusted me. Most people stayed six months to a year before they moved on. Janie spent her first three weeks trying to slit her wrists open again, so four men had to sleep on the grounds in case they had to restrain her. It was the only time I'd seen men at Countryside. The rehabilitation center is a female retreat set in the hills of New England, far from hospitals and skyscrapers and everything that made me want to die.

Countryside was where rich, severely mentally ill women could go to instead of an institution. Only ten patients could stay at a time. The philosophy was that fresh air and working on the land were better solutions for mental illness than a bunch of pills to swallow. And we had all signed the paperwork saying we wanted this treatment, that we preferred this path. But once signed, we couldn't leave until our individual doctors agreed that we were ready to reintegrate back into the world.

This was the same world that drove us all insane. The very same world that pushed us to the edge of society, left us clinging to the last bit of light in our lives. Whenever someone new came to Countryside, they considered it a fresh start. They enjoyed the gardening, the cooking, and living off the land. They liked riding the horses and tending to the farm animals. But after a few weeks, they grew restless. Countryside didn't have cell phones or internet access. There's no way to tell what celebrities were posting on social media or what trend was sweeping the beauty industry. There was no shopping for clothes, no YouTube to watch. There were only open skies, acres of fields, and each other.

I PLACED A PLATE of bread on the table and looked at Ms. Evans, the team leader at Countryside.

"Where's Alicia?" I asked. She was my second favorite to Janie.

"She's out in the garden," said May, a yoga influencer from Santa Monica. "Last time I saw her, she was cradling a chicken."

I stepped out to find her. Alicia was sweet, a girl who was easily forgotten because of her aversion to drama. Her whole life, all she wanted was to have children. When she and her husband were ready, at the age of thirty-two, she learned that she couldn't conceive. She never gave a full picture of what specifically led her to Countryside, but one had to only be in her presence for a few moments to see the blurry line she walked between whimsical and delusional. When I found her out back, she was humming to herself, and she was indeed cradling a chicken.

"Time for dinner," I said, brushing some dirt off her bandana.

"You'd never kill these babies, would you?" Alicia let the chicken down while it clucked.

"I don't have it in me to kill a chicken," I said. "Come on. You know the meat all comes from the market."

"Hmm," was all she said as we walked back. The chilly spring air held enough promise that warmer weather was coming. We washed our hands and I returned to the table, entering a conversation about the farmers' market.

"She goes every week and we never get to choose our own stuff," May said, eyeing me as I dished myself some food.

"Leola has been here a long time," Ms. Evans murmured. "We've been over this. She goes to the market because it's difficult for me to carry those bags now that my carpal tunnel has come back."

I nodded as audible groans erupted around me. This would not be the last time we talked about this.

"I'm just saying that if we were to have our own booth at the market, I could sell my arrangements," May said. "I think they're getting really good."

"It's true," one of the older women said. "They're very beautiful." They weren't.

May had taken up flower arrangement this month and was convinced she was good at it because no one in her life had ever told her that she should try and improve. She told us this herself during group therapy after chronicling her failed career as first an actress, then a singer, and finally, a comedian. I would have imagined her to be quite funny, actually, if she were very drunk. But she'd abused alcohol enough to show up at Countryside, so her vices had become narrower. Yoga and flowers. That had become May's life.

"If you stay a year, you might be able to go to the market with Leola," Ms. Evans said to May. "But we won't have a booth at the market. No. Too much risk. Outside influence and all that."

"But—" May started.

"No," Ms. Bolton stated firmly, and that was that.

After dinner I sat out back, staring out at the March sky. I rubbed my hands together to stay warm. Janie joined me, which she usually did to be exempt from cleaning dishes.

"You ever miss cigarettes?" Janie asked.

"I never smoked," I said.

Janie laughed. "What *did* you do?"

THAT NIGHT I RETIRED to my room and felt the world tilt. There was no way for me to know what was coming, but I like to think that maybe I could feel the universe click out of alignment. Perhaps I'd just been picking up on micro expressions. Either way, it made me regress and I began thinking about things before Countryside. I closed my eyes and remembered the way that life used to be, all those years ago. Me, at three o'clock in the morning, staring out the window at the city lights.

Staring into an abyss.

It had started slowly. Sleepless nights turned into a symphony of missed work days, drinking Nyquil from the bottle, napping through the afternoon, and waking up to see the sun had set. Panic crept in and paralyzed me until I forgot how to function properly.

I saw many doctors after that. They asked me about my stress levels and if I had a history of abuse. I didn't, but both of my parents were lifelong hypochondriacs. They convinced me to do sleep studies, to wear a watch that monitored my REM cycle.

Trouble sleeping turned into never sleeping. I'd go days without it. I walked bleary-eyed through the evenings, stumbling around in the dark like a phantom. When the exhaustion caught up with me, it pounced like a predator, and I gave in, collapsing onto my sofa where I remained for ten hours at a time.

I'd been poked and prodded. I'd been prescribed pills. Many different pills. All different colors, all with different side effects. When I was officially fired, the relief nearly knocked me sideways. I hadn't considered that it was the job that kept me up. I hadn't even hated the job, I just disliked the monotonous droning of the workplace. I loathed how little I saw the sun. I went, day after day, understanding that it paid my rent, that it put food in my fridge. Each day was the same. I couldn't escape the existential dread that slipped under my pillow each night. *Is this it?* I would wonder. *Is this all there is?* In the end, the idea of being institutionalized was actually better than the idea of putting on my work trousers one more time.

At Countryside, I'd never slept so well. With my eyes still closed, I thought about Janie, about Alicia and her chickens, about May and the flower arrangements. Insomnia was the name of an old, difficult acquaintance. This time, the abyss that swallowed me up was that of slumber, and I greeted it every night as a close friend.

THE NEXT MORNING I slept in, which was unusual for me. I walked downstairs, groggy, taking in the blinding sunshine.

"Hey," one of the new, young girls called to me from a rocking chair. "You missed May's class."

"Shit," I said. I opened the fridge to find some juice.

"She's in a bad mood now," the girl said.

I closed the fridge and went to the back of the house.

The homestead was modest, but it was newly built with one side facing endless fields. The other side, the back of the home, faced the mountains that gently rolled down into a valley. May liked to hold Sunday yoga and meditation there. It was our version of worship. And May was not so easy to get along with. But giving each person a bit of encouragement usually helped them on their journey. Also, the quickest way to get May out of Countryside was to make her feel empowered, which she did best when she was leading us in yoga.

"How was the class?" I asked, watching her roll up a few mats.

"Great," she said, clipped. She stood and adjusted her tiny shorts. "Everyone else was there."

"I'm feeling a bit off," I said. "Maybe I'm catching a cold."

"Sounds like something your parents would say," May said, smiling sweetly, though she knew it was a poisoned arrow. May had a nice way of looking polite and still making you hate her. She'd spent five years being a wellness influencer online while secretly abusing booze and prescription drugs. I liked to remind myself that she wasn't as mindful as she pretended to be. Still, I cursed myself for sharing any part of my past around her.

"Where's everyone else?" I asked, doing my best to sound civil.

"They're all outside. Trying to see if the ground has thawed, I swear it hasn't. It's so fucking cold here."

"Right," I said.

"Janie went for a ride," May said.

"Again?" I looked out at the view behind her, at the rolling mountains and hillside. "She goes so often now."

I put on my heavy coat and walked out into the garden and found that everyone, including Ms. Evans, was out poking at the frozen ground. "Give it a few weeks," Ms. Evans said. "Soon, it'll be mild, and then it'll be summer before you know it. Happens every year. The miracle of life, the cycle of death and rebirth . . ."

I walked past them and down one of the trails through a meadow. The tall grass was brown and dry from a long winter. Everything was wet.

It's true, there hadn't been much that I'd done before Countryside. I didn't have an interesting life like some of these women.

I didn't have a bunch of followers online. I didn't run a fashion empire, like Janie did before she found her husband cheating on her with a twenty-year-old. Some of the women were communications moguls, or they had several degrees from fancy schools, or they traveled for work and saw every continent. I'd simply spent my life existing.

I couldn't wait to be on my own, and once I'd finally done it, I was shocked to find that I was unfulfilled. It felt like taking years to crawl out of a hole only to find myself teetering on the edge of a cliff. There was no satisfaction. There was no safety net. My degrees were behind me. I was bored with literature, which had been my one true love. I was sick of being invited to parties. One therapist listened to me prattle on about everything that I didn't care about anymore because I was too scared of my lack of sleep. "Have you considered," the therapist said, "that you might just be very bored of your life?"

Apparently, I had been life threateningly bored of it.

At Countryside, the trails loop around to the most beautiful areas of the grounds. One path led over a bridge with a brook. Another weaved through the forest. My favorite path went through the meadows and turned into a boardwalk that hovered over the wetlands. No one had tried to escape from Countryside because we were so isolated from everything else. There was nowhere else to go. I never thought about leaving, anyway.

I stood at the edge of the boardwalk and watched the different birds. I stayed quiet, and I marveled at a Great Blue Heron. Two Eared Grebes paddled away from me in the murky water. A little gray and white bird that I couldn't identify chirped a little tune. And in the distance, a dark spot on my outing, was a murder of crows.

I couldn't ever seem to avoid them, the dark and clever things. I remembered watching similar crows in the city, the way they perched on the edges of buildings and stared. They were the only things that I saw at Countryside that I related to the city, to the old life I used to live. They were pecking at each other, so wrapped up in their own world that they didn't notice me scowling at them.

I made my way back up the boardwalk and walked on, farther north than I usually do. The crows had unnerved me with their stupid beady eyes. It was then that I saw the horse tied up in the distance, much further up the path. It was Janie's horse, the one she always liked to ride. I jogged a bit, thinking that something might be amiss. It was when I got closer that I stopped and quieted. From behind some large bushes I could hear the unmistakable sounds of lovemaking.

I still quietly walked forward. I felt like I was in a dream. The horse sniffed at me and I gave it a warning glance. Janie's boots were tossed against a tree, and behind the bushes, a blanket had been laid out. I'm not sure why I did it, but I continued walking until I saw them, their bodies twisted together while they made hushed noises of pleasure. Something jumped out at me then: a tattoo snaking around the man's arm. I turned and walked away as soon as I saw it, not looking at the horse as I passed. Once I got a bit farther, I ran, all the way down the path and through the meadow until the garden came into view.

I stopped before anyone could see me and forced myself to breathe, in and out. Then I went to the shed to get one of the heavy picnic blankets. I found a spot near Alicia, who was brushing a goat. I lay out under the sun, despite the cold air on my skin and in my lungs.

"Were you running?" Alicia asked, peeking down at me.

"Just a bit," I said. "I think I'm out of shape."

"Me too," Alicia said. She smiled warmly at me. "But I still never go to yoga class."

DURING GROUP THERAPY, A psychologist drove in once a week to listen to our tales of woe. We sat in a circle, maneuvering the rocking chairs so that we could all see each other.

"What was your challenge of the week?" asked Leslie, the psychologist. She was a short, middle-aged woman with a round nose, and she never seemed to like us that much. She was the only professional I'd done therapy with that had such a cold demeanor, but she got away with it because she was passing off our information as data. They were not confessions of family dysfunction or admissions of jealousy, of anger at our best friends who were off living their normal lives. She probably recorded these stories as showing signs of instability, low self-worth, symptoms of personality disorders. I guessed that she used clinical words for our honest confessions.

"I'm getting really good at the flower arrangements," May said. "But I'm not allowed to sell them at the market so no one even sees them."

"Perhaps it's enough that your friends here can admire them," Leslie said to May expectantly. We all blinked at each other in response. I wanted to laugh.

To my astonishment, May shut up. She didn't fight or whine as usual. She tucked her legs under herself where she sat and she stared at the ground.

I felt Janie's eyes on me, so I looked up and held her gaze. She knew, somehow. She knew that I knew. Maybe I'd been too obvious with my spying. Embarrassment flooded my veins, and to escape her scrutiny, I spontaneously raised my hand.

"Yes, Leola," Leslie said. "What was your challenge of the week?"

I was astonished that I'd elected myself to speak but I was desperate to stop thinking of the horse tied up, of the crows haunting the wetlands. I wanted to surrender some truth to the group in exchange for infringing on Janie's privacy. I cleared my throat.

"I've been thinking about my problems with sleeping," I said.

"Do you still have issues with your sleeping?" Leslie asked. I could hear the doubt in her voice. I hadn't talked to her about my troubles in years.

"No," I said. "Not anymore."

"You're just, what, remembering them? The issues you used to have?"

I nodded, red-faced. I'd been there longer than anyone else, so I rarely shared my past with this group of people. Not even with Janie. Not with Alicia, either.

"How's it feel when you remember it?" Leslie asked me.

"It feels like—" I swallowed. My mouth had gone dry. "I can't believe that was what my life was like."

"So you feel better now?" Leslie wasn't looking at me. She was making notes, her stubby fingers drumming against her knee.

In truth, here's how it felt: I'd never felt so good in all my life as I did at Countryside. I'd grown up in the city. I passed bodegas and homeless people and blaring car horns every day. My parents caged me in their grand home that had been passed down to them, and this was my prison. They closed the curtains and asked doctors to come and assess us for diseases that we didn't have. The curtains didn't bother me; I hated to look outside and see the chaos out there.

I despised every reminder of the city. I went to school and buried myself in the farthest corner of the library. The old building was made of stone so thick that I couldn't hear anything outside. I moved from school to home and back again, day after day, only surviving to escape to the library and its dim lighting. I pored over stories that took place in wide open spaces. Romance stories where people fell in love and slept naked in each other's beds. I wondered what that would be like, and I never expected to find out. I thought, for most of my childhood, that I was going to die young, as my parents were always sick and the doctor visited me frequently to monitor me.

When I was old enough to trade school for my job, and my parents' home for an apartment, I was exposed to the world. I could hide no longer. I had no respite. I had no energy to visit any library where I could pretend to be somewhere else. I only had my memory of that school library, of the time in my life that was formative and was now over. I cried only when I thought of those days in school, of my escapist coping mechanisms. Yes, I had been miserable, but it was a misery that was comfortable to me.

Then the sleeping troubles started. I regularly felt the promise of sleep weighing over my body like a heavy cloak, threatening to wrap around me and squeeze until I suffocated. Then the sleeping pills. Then, finally, an overdose, and a stern talk with my parents. To Countryside I went.

Leaving my apartment was like shedding old skin. I watched the garbage tossing around the busy street, and that turned into suburban towns, and that turned into a highway. The landscape opened up at one point and mountains greeted me on either side, valleys dipping far below the interstate.

I'd never left the city. I was never going back.

"I feel better now," I said to Leslie. The heat left my cheeks. Sometimes it's good, I think, to remember how long your road has been. It's a tonic for self-consciousness.

After group therapy, I sat in my room with large socks that I'd knit the month before. I was drinking chamomile tea. When I tell you that life was very good for me, I mean it sincerely. Most of my nights were spent this way and I never tired of it. I wanted to grow old and die looking at those same mountains.

Janie knocked on my door. She shut it when she came into the room. "I saw you," she said.

I stared at her, amused at the hilarity of the whole thing. "No," I said. "I saw you."

"Don't you say a word—"

"Why would I?" I sipped my tea and did my best to make my expression calm, but really, anxiety was gnawing at my brain. I'd seen the man with the tattoo once, holding Janie down as she writhed and fought those first weeks. He was one of the guards. And we weren't meant to interact with them, which meant that if Janie was caught, our entire ecosystem might collapse.

"Why are you messing around with him?" I asked.

"Because I'm bored," she whispered. Janie acted the tough cookie, but I could see the cracks sometimes. She was insecure. Her husband cheated on her with a girl who couldn't even legally drink, and when Janie asked for a divorce, he didn't fight her on it. I couldn't imagine dealing with that level of rejection. Janie's confidence was built on a house of cards, and now she was stuck here at a homestead with goats and a bunch of other women who had tried to kill themselves. So yes, I understood why she might have wanted attention from anyone she could get it from.

"I hate it here," Janie said. "I miss my old life and I want to leave."

"You'll be out soon enough," I said.

"No, I fucking won't. I told you. My doctor is a huge dick. He gets off on keeping me here. He knows—he wants me to beg him to leave, by the way—he *knows* that I'm better and I should be able to go home. I don't belong here."

"What's so bad about staying here?" I asked.

She seethed, teeth clenched. "Leola, you're so fucking high and mighty. You're the best at healing your trauma—"

"I never said that," I said.

"You'd never leave, if you had the chance. You're going to stay here forever because you had a sad life. You have nothing to go home to."

I said nothing. She was right, anyway.

THE NEXT NIGHT I went to Ms. Evans' room and locked the door behind me. "Hey," I said. "Everyone's asleep."

"Great," Ms. Evans said, and she took off her glasses and rubbed her eyes. "How's everyone?"

"Fine," I said, though it wasn't quite true. Things had been strange since I'd found out about Janie's secret. But I didn't think it was important enough to share.

"Your mother called." Ms. Evans stared at me, her eyes so sharp and familiar.

"What'd you tell her?" I asked.

"I didn't. I said you were going to call her back."

"Oh." I shifted my weight and the floorboards creaked beneath me. "Okay, then."

"You're not going to call, are you?"

I just looked out the window and sighed.

"I hate doing this, you know," Ms. Evans said. "It's been so long that I've played the middleman. They're worried about you."

"But I'm fine here," I said. "I'm happy. You can tell them."

"It's not my job to have those conversations with them. I don't like coming up with excuses for you, either." She shook her head. "I hate lying to my sister."

I thought about my mother, about how similar they looked. Ms. Evans was actually Sadie Evans, my aunt Sadie. And Sadie was hardy, able to pull vegetables and weeds out of the ground, formidable enough to run a house full of ten suicidal women. My mother, on the other hand, shook from the drafty house she lived in, and she always seemed to shrivel inward like a late-autumn leaf.

"I'll find time when the landline is free," I said, though I couldn't actually imagine what I might say to my mother.

"You can use my cell phone," Sadie said. "What? No one will ask anything. These girls are all so wrapped up in their own misery that they don't see a damn thing."

"These women are here for a reason," I said. "They're running from their own demons."

"That's fine," Sadie said. "All I'm saying is that you need to call your mother." She stood and went to her bed, her hand lingering on the lamp beside her. "Good night," she said.

I WOKE UP, COUGHING. The room was hot and my breathing was ragged. Immediately my eyes stung and I blindly reached for the light. Once the room was lit I could see thick smoke hanging around the ceiling.

Shit, I thought, and I had no idea what to do. They sometimes did fire safety drills in school and that had been so long ago that you might as well have been asking me to do long division. I rolled to the ground and found it easier to breathe there. Crawling to the window, I pried it open and felt the hot air suck out of it and into the freezing night. I gathered some strength then and pushed the window up, higher and higher. I moved to the other window and did the same. I took a deep breath next to the open window but still felt a heaviness in my chest. I coughed, hard, until I heard the door behind me.

Then hands on my wrists, steering me out and down the hall. It was Janie, her hair down but still sleek and straight. I let her steer me past the bedrooms, which were all filled with smoke as well, and down the stairs.

Shit, I kept thinking. *I hope this is a horrible dream.*

It was worse downstairs. "What happened?" I yelled to Janie. There were flames licking around the fireplace and kitchen, eating up some of the rocking chairs. My eyes were glued there, unable to comprehend what was happening.

"Something set it off," Janie yelled. She wouldn't look me in the eye.

"What, though?" I wracked my brain trying to think of what we might have left on that caught fire. Janie was pushing me harshly toward the back door. We had to jump over a few areas of angry, red flames that bit at my ankles.

The heat inside was enough to make me sweat, my flannel shirt was drenched. But once outside, I was freezing. I realized my shoes were inside. Everything was inside. Janie brushed by me to join the group of women who were staring up at the fire.

That was when I finally woke up. I properly woke up and looked at the beautiful thing before me that was devolving into nothing. I whipped around and counted everyone, then counted again. We were missing people. "Who else is inside?!" I yelled.

To my relief, I saw Sadie walking up from the shed. She was holding her cell phone and she caught my eye. "Two more are coming out," she said to me. As she said it I heard the kitchen door swing and two of the younger women stumbled out with May, who was leading them like a war hero.

"What the hell happened?" I yelled again, but no one seemed to care enough to respond. They were either pacing back and forth with

Sadie, who was green in the face, or they were staring up at the building while it burned.

I could feel Sadie next to me, her arm brushing against mine. "Someone set the fire," she whispered.

"What?" I looked around at the group and I shook my head.

"I know it," she said. "I heard some commotion last night and I thought they were just hungry and making a snack. I almost went downstairs."

"Who was it?" I asked.

"Hard to say." Sadie's eyes were moist. It might have been from the smoke.

We stayed like that, in a trance, for a long while. Then a few wooden beams snapped, making us jump, and the fire poured down the side of the house.

"Okay," I yelled, clapping. "We need to get the animals away from the building. Right?" They all stared at me. "Right?! Jesus, fucking move! Alicia?"

She appeared next to me. "I'll walk them further back." Her trance-like demeanor was gone and replaced with determination.

"Good. Take a few girls with you." I looked around at the women who were sitting close to the house, staring up at the flames in a mesmerized fashion. "Hey, you're too close," I said. "Get up. Come on, we all need to get out of here."

"My phone's in there," one of them said, as if she just realized she forgot someone's birthday.

"We aren't supposed to have phones here," Sadie said disapprovingly.

"There's nothing in that building that we're saving," I said to them. "So back up. Let's move to the shed."

"I called the police," Sadie said as we watched the women move toward the shed with some animals in tow. "I don't know how it happened."

There was movement in the distance, far away from the house.

There were two beams of light dancing off the trees. They caught my eye, the same way the crows in the meadow had.

"Is there room in the barn for all of us and the animals?" I asked.

"Yeah," Sadie said. "If I go and clear some stuff out to make room."

"Go ahead and do that," I said. "I'll meet up with you in a second."

I walked until Sadie disappeared into the barn, and then I ran down the path, my arms and fingers freezing from the cold. A few times I slipped on the frozen mud along the path and cursed. But I caught up with them eventually.

"Janie," I wheezed, and a few of the flashlights landed on me.

Janie, May, and two other patients were standing in a clearing of trees. They all watched me with icy expressions.

"I'm sorry," Janie said. "But I've got to get out of here. We've got someone waiting on the other side. I just can't stay here—"

"Don't," I said, holding up my hand while I caught my breath. "I don't care. I don't care."

"Why'd you run all this way then?" May hissed. "You're gonna tattle on us?"

I laughed and shook my head. "No, May, I don't give a shit if you stay or go." I hadn't been so angry in years. Maybe in my entire life.

"Good," she said, lifting her chin. "Because we're leaving."

I stepped forward and slapped Janie across the face hard. She drew back, shocked, and then watched me as she held her chin.

"Why couldn't you have just gone in the night?" I asked. "You didn't need to do this. Look at this!" I screamed. I motioned back behind me, and the view of the homestead—of my *home*—nearly crushed me.

"We needed a way out," Janie said, voice soft.

"You might have just walked out and taken your idiots with you," I said, breathing heavily. "Now what are we supposed to do?"

"We don't care!" May said, and she put her hand on Janie's shoulder. "Come on, before they see us leave. The police are coming."

"You're right. You don't care. So go," I said, and I took a few steps back. My socks were soaked through and I couldn't feel my toes. "Please get out of here. You were right. You don't belong here. Especially not now."

Janie's eyes flickered between me and the fire that blazed behind me. Then she turned and went, sleek hair and all.

I walked my way past the boardwalk and the riding trails. Never before had I considered how fragile my paradise was. All these years that I was hiding away, I was taking for granted each day that I woke up and felt at peace. There was no question in my mind, we would rebuild. I would help. I'd nail up every board of the new house if I had to. This new sense of purpose swelled inside my chest. The smoke streaked against the sky as a reminder of the threat ahead of me, but I refused to see the burning homestead as anything besides an eventual second chance.

I burst into the barn and greeted the rest of the women that were sitting inside. "Sadie," I said, "let me see your phone."

I walked back out and watched the flames corrode my bedroom where I had been only a half hour before. I imagined myself in my bed still, the fire roasting me and burning my skin to a crisp. I guess things could've been worse.

I swiped at the phone clumsily until I could dial the number. It rang in unison with sirens that were singing from a few miles away. The kitchen collapsed on itself then, a ball of smoke erupting from inside. The only thing left that I could see was the stained-glass window that gleamed like a martyr in battle.

"Hello?"

"Mom," I said.

"Leola—"

"I'm sorry," I said. "I never called."

There was silence as a firetruck came into view. The sirens were so loud that I almost couldn't hear her. "What's that?"

"Some problems at Countryside," I said. "But it's going to be okay."

"Are you hurt?" she asked, and I pictured her by the phone, looking around with wide eyes as she gripped the phone.

"I'm good, Mom," I said. "I'm really good. Can you hear me? I mean it. I'm happy."

"But what's all that going on?" she asked, her voice nearly drowned out by all the sirens that were coming to save us.

"It's going to be okay," I said, my eyes on the stained glass. "I love you."

I hung up and watched the firefighters jump off their truck. When I turned around I saw the flashlights in the distance, already much farther into the forest. Prisoners that were flying away. Let them go, then. Back into the world that had hurt them before. I couldn't imagine what it was that they were running toward, but I had no desire to ever see it again.

The Witch

Katherine Royce

ONCE THERE WAS A WITCH.

Once, longer ago than now, for at least a day, she had dreamed of being a princess. But as she grew past teenage fantasies and into womanhood, she realized there weren't many job opportunities for sturdy, plain princesses with sarcastic eyebrows and a slight but perpetual smirk. And besides, the few times she'd needed rescuing, she'd grown bored within a few minutes and gone ahead and rescued herself.

As she grew older and acquired more stray cats and hand-fed ravens, and her knowledge of herblore grew deeper and her patience for small talk grew shallower, the villagers began whispering. And then one crisp autumn day, a prince arrived and said he would cleanse them of evil.

As he bound her hands and cast her into the river, she mused that he was not as handsome as one might have hoped. Then she watched the world shimmer away in a stream of bubbles as her breath escaped her, and she sank to the bottom.

She grew bored lying in the silt waiting to drown, so she freed her hands and let the river carry her away to the sea. It was easy to find a nice cave if you didn't mind sharing with an octopus, and there were always merfolk who needed a poultice or tincture. And someone needed to talk sense into sea princesses suffering their first heartbreak. After all, teenage girls can make silly choices without guidance.

And she lived, ever after.

Hips

Laurel Maxwell

After Lucille Clifton

Hips, how you hover in orbit every time I walk.

Sashaying down the hard cement of this city by the sea.

Propelling me down wooded paths,

up mountain scree. On roads familiar and obscure.

Motion your nexus of control, one summer you quit in protest.

Refusing to move in the direction I wanted.

Hips, you kept me humble.

Relearning how to move fluid as a weaver's nimble hands.

It became the year of watching dew collect on a spider's web,

observing ducklings moving linearly down the river.

Of seeing the sun rise in the cleavage of mountains.

A tart taste of salsa made from our bounty of tomatoes.

The daily hum and *thunk* of the refrigerator.

The weight you carry settling fine as dust upon this bodily frame.

Hips, you kept me stable.

As we learned how to wear masks and conserve water.

As heat combusted into spontaneous flame across this tinderbox state.

As the world kept forever spinning like a top.

Rebecca's Piano

Diane Allerdyce

IT'S FRIDAY NIGHT, AND THE KIDS AND I HAVE JUST RETURNED FROM A WALK along the beach. The sky was hazy, tinged with purple above the bright corridor of moonlight on the ocean's surface. Afterward we went to Doc's for a root beer float and sat on the patio across from Old School Square. The loudspeakers above us projected a crackly Jackie DeShannon voice insisting that what the world needs now is love. There's truth in that, I reflected, as long as love is really love, right?

"What are you thinking about, Mom?" Brenda asked.

"Yeah, Mom," Mike echoed. "What are you thinking about?"

I pulled my gaze away from another family I'd been watching at an adjacent table and smiled into the eyes of my own two children, now ten and twelve years old. What I'd been thinking about all evening was the summer three years ago when I learned to define my boundaries and heal myself from emotional pain by playing the piano.

THAT WAS THE SUMMER of 1991, when I was thirty-three. It's not that I learned to play that summer, for I'd played off and on since the age of six. I'd never crossed a certain threshold in my playing from passable to good, but I knew how to get around a bit on a keyboard. So, no, it's not that I taught myself to play, or that I learned something truly new that summer. But I did learn to draw on a skill I'd set aside, and I learned to fashion out of my playing a shield against loneliness and fear—even against the anxiety that had plagued me since childhood. Best of all, I was able to cultivate my confusion and anger into a kind of bonsai art form—channeling its bigness, its overwhelmingness, into neat little tunes—Bach sonatas running brook-like through my fingers, Janice Joplin or Rolling Stones arrangements from an old anthology of seventies hits emerging at my fingertips like packaged fruit. I've since come to think of my anger as a tool I used to dispel certain (dis)illusions, but it was partly anger that served me that summer. I found in my relationship with Robert plenty of fuel for it.

We'd broken up again for the seventh time in two years. He'd taken to stopping by for sex, and I'd taken to jumping at the offer as if I had no other options. The fact is I had other options—a married man whose wife, he said, was like a sister to him, and a recent prospect from the personal ads in the freebie newspaper that appeared at the edge of the pothole in my driveway each Thursday afternoon around five o'clock, just as I would likely be climbing the walls of my children's rooms and pouring my first—usually of two or three—glasses of wine that I'd drink alone each evening after the kids were in bed. I was grateful that Robert didn't come by when they were home, except to pick them up. No, it was only while they were safely at camp that he'd come knocking.

My emotional life was a perpetual maelstrom. "No, thank you" was something I thought about saying only three rounds into a terrible argument, *after* sex, when he had turned mean and was blaming me for trapping him into sleeping with him. He'd accuse me of disregarding his wishes by seducing him, by begging for his company and making him feel so guilty on the phone that he had no choice but to come over. It's true that I'd called him a few times. Sometimes I couldn't tell whether it was he or I who had inflicted neediness or guilt on the other.

"Olivia," Robert would say—lowering his voice on the phone when I'd called him "just to chat" or "just to say hi." "Olivia," he'd ask just after that lull that meant the conversation was about to end (as if it really had any business getting started in the first place), "are you missing me?" My resistance would instantly melt away at that one. I'd picture his dark gray eyes becoming a little droopy and the smile lines that run from the sides of his nose down to the outer edges of his mustache taking on that lovely upward curve that made my stomach take a little leap. I was a complete sap, I'd remind myself at times like that. But in that one second the inside of my arms would relax from the armpits to the elbow, and I'd say, "You know I do," lowering my voice to match his.

"Want me to stop by in the morning?" he'd ask, and then, purely as a formality, would inquire what time I'd be back from taking the kids to camp. He knew the answer, but he liked, I suppose, to pretend that he wasn't their father and that I was his mistress rather than his ex-wife. Or quite possibly, that is what I liked to pretend. The game did have a certain attraction, and I'd hang up the phone able to go on with my business of reading a story to Brenda and Mike, throwing in a load of laundry, catching up on correspondence—you know, the usual stuff—all the while pushing down the little jack-in-the-box that was my wiser self, my Goddess Within, so that I could ignore the warning that I was succumbing to behavior from which I'd suffer by noon tomorrow. Forget you, I'd say brusquely to the Goddess-in-the-Box. I have plenty of time for you tomorrow. Then I'd go about my business, enjoying the little pinpricks of anticipation running down the backs of my thighs as I imagined the lovemaking I'd enjoy the next morning. After all, it was never more than once a week; at my ripe age of thirty-three, that was infrequently enough that my nipples would rise at the mere thought of sex.

As the July Fourth weekend approached, though, I'd begun to feel uneasy with our arrangement. Robert and I'd been divorced for nearly ten months, over half of those in some kind of reunion or re-estrangement. Twice weekly since our divorce the previous September, and separately from our private morning rendezvous, he'd seen the children. Once was always on Tuesday evening for dinner and a video in the motorhome he'd acquired by selling the sailboat he got in the settlement. For nearly ten months he'd lived in that vehicle, parking it at the local campground between the K-Mart and the animal shelter on Federal Highway. "Guess how much?" he'd asked me one morning while the kids were at camp, propping himself up on one elbow on my futon mattress as I twirled his slightly graying chest hair with one finger and wondered somewhat absently whether I had time to work out to my aerobics video. (Distraction, I realized later, had become a defense, one I'd cultivated purposely to avoid being hurt by the same characteristic in others.)

It was summer, and I was officially off from my teaching job at the school I'd privately nicknamed Wayside Academy, a private college for students who might otherwise have gone by the wayside of the college track. I liked to go in for a few hours now and then to organize my files, check on book orders, or otherwise feel useful and at least a little bit connected to some kind of structured system outside the family of which I was now sole structurer. I was thinking about these things when I gradually became aware that, still propped up on one elbow, Robert was looking at me.

"What?" I demanded.

"What do you mean 'What'?" he teased, kissing me. "Why are you so spaced out? I asked you three times what you were thinking about!"

It was true that I was often absentminded. Had I answered him after he told me the price of his motor home? I couldn't remember. It was no wonder Brenda and Mike liked to tease me about being spaced out. Had they gotten the term from Robert? Maybe he had gotten it from them. A bit defensively, I hoped they hadn't in their innocent chatter given him some kind of weapon to use against me should we ever have differences over custody. Not that he'd want the responsibility of the children but . . . What was I thinking? I'd just made wild passionate love (or something in that category) to this man. Why should I get paranoid now?

"I have a lot on my mind!" I said.

"Oh, is that right?" Already I could feel him pulling in his energy and beginning to make plans to get up. This was probably not the time to ask him to accompany me and the kids to my sister's house in Orlando for the Fourth of July weekend. "What do you have on your mind?"

I turned away, slipping my legs over the side of the futon. Might as well make the first move. "Oh, you know," I said a little more sarcastically than I'd planned, "the kids, the dog, the station wagon, how white my laundry is compared to the lady's next door—that kind of thing."

I stood up, keeping my back to him as I began to dress. I felt ridiculous keeping my spine so stoic while slipping violet satin underwear over my thighs and bum. Nevertheless, I was determined not to sacrifice any self-respect. I gathered my violet satin bra and denim shorts in one hand and lifted my chin as I made my way to the bathroom. I began to hum.

As I reached the bathroom door something hit the wall next to it. The thud was followed in quick succession by another. I paused at the door, not turning. "You forgot your shoes," he said.

I turned, smiling. "Why, thank you, honey." His face turned a little gray; the smile line from his nose to his mustache had deepened. His chest muscles twitched a bit as he rose from the futon. I ducked into the bathroom and locked the door, leaving my leather sandals where they'd landed. I knew he'd be gone by the time I emerged.

"Mom!" Brenda called loudly that evening from the bathtub two feet away.

"What, honey? I'm right here!"

"Mom, that was the fourth time I called you!" Her little face was red with exasperation.

"I'm sorry, honey. I didn't hear you."

* * *

ROBERT HADN'T LEFT WHEN I emerged from the bathroom dressed in my workout clothes. To my surprise he was sitting on the bed, fully dressed.

"What are you doing?" I asked.

"Waiting." My stomach took a little jump as I guessed that he'd come to some kind of decision. I was right. "We need to talk," he said.

A bodily memory of exhaustion gave me an instant warning headache. My throat tightened, reminding me to avoid an emotional scene that would wreck the remainder of the day. I wavered between summoning my recently dissipated anger to my defense and surrendering to my old habit of throwing away all my goals for the day at the slightest suggestion. "I'm not sure I do, actually, Robert," I said, with what I hoped sounded like a firm resolve. Silly me—to think I could sound firm with a wishy-washy sentence like that. I sat across from him on the bed and pulled on a sock and sneaker, then reached for the other foot.

Robert stood up as if he had weights on his shoulders. As if to take a mental detour, my mind flashed to the ankle weights I kept above the dryer in the laundry room. I should remember to wear them during my workout this time.

"Olivia," Robert said slowly, like a parent disappointed in a wayward child for whom he'd been waiting up, rehearsing the speech he'd to give upon that child's return. "I'm sorry you are too busy to face the reality of what has been happening here." He turned sorrowfully toward me, one hand on the bedpost, the other in his pocket. He was dressed in his navy suit pants that made him look taller—and fitter—than he was. His white cotton shirt was perfectly starched, and his silk tie just slightly irreverent with its green, not quite reefer-looking leaves against a blue background. Maybe it was wishful thinking on my part that in his stodginess Robert would unknowingly offend an authority figure with a countercultural symbol inadvertently adopted. But no—those leaves were clearly ivy.

Suddenly, the realization that he was seeing someone else hit me. It started at my scalp above my neck and ran down my spine, skipping when it got to the coccyx to my hips and weakening knees. I drew in a breath. "Don't say that, Rob."

"It has to be said. We both know it."

"Look—let's just forget my moodiness, today, okay? I have PMS. And to tell you the truth, I've just been nervous about asking you to my sister's for the Fourth." I leaned a knee on the bed.

He lowered his chin and spoke to the floor. "What are you talking about, Olivia? God!"

"About the Fourth of July! I've been wishing we could spend it like a real family again—you and me and Brenda and Mike. Why shouldn't we?"

"Because we're not a family anymore and haven't been for a long time. Where have you been?

"I just thought—"

"What exactly did you think?"

"That we were trying to get back together."

"For Christ's sake, Olivia, I'm with someone else! You had to have known that. As a matter of fact, I'm spending the Fourth with her and *her* sister's family."

It was no use. Yet above the ringing in my ears I heard the continuation of my ridiculous voice. "How would I have known that?" I slumped to a seated position on the bed.

I BELIEVE ROBERT ACTUALLY threw his hands up at that point. I didn't see him, but I sensed it in the way he slumped, in turn, to sit on the bed. We must have looked like bookends turned out the wrong way, two faces pointing in opposite directions at opposite walls of the same room. His voice sounded resigned, as if to my stupidity.

"Why?" he asked almost gently. "Why would we be meeting like this in the mornings if we were getting back together? Why wouldn't we have just been meeting like normal people, after work, having dinner, playing with the kids, hitting the sack? Really, Ollie, you knew, didn't you?"

"I thought we were protecting the kids . . . you know, until we were sure."

"Protecting them from what?"

"1 don't know—false hope or something."

"1 don't understand you at all. First you tell me you don't want to be married. Then, as soon as I've gone through the hell of that and found someone who does want me, you call me back, over and over, trying to make up your mind."

It was true, I have to admit to myself now. But I wouldn't have admitted it to him for anything. "*My* mind?" I protested.

"Yes, *your* mind!" Robert rose. "But that's not the problem. The problem is your seductive little body and the way you use it to play with my mind!"

Said in a different tone, the same words might have turned me on. Now, however, he'd retreated to anger, summoning his mean streak as a weapon. Yet instead of the anger I usually went to in response, I felt something different. The pretense was over. When he left a short time later, acting a bit apologetic as if he wanted to leave the proverbial door unlatched if not a tad bit open, I knew it would be a while until his next visit.

As I SAT ON the closed toilet lid that night and realized it had taken Brenda three or four attempts to get my attention even though I sat only two feet away from her, my head ached, my throat ached, and it very truly seemed that my very heart was beginning to ache, as cliché as that sounds. I think I also realized then that I'd truly be a single mom for the foreseeable future. Celibacy would be hard enough, but it was the aloneness that hit me with unexpected force as I watched the water swirl down the drain and as I reached tenderly for the little girl whose hair extended into rivulets of streaming water down her back.

I STARTED PLAYING THE piano again almost by accident, except that by now I believe I can truly say, in spite of my tendency to make fun of such hokeyness, that there are no accidents. After Robert's departure that day, an emptiness had expanded inside my chest as the reality of my situation sank in. I'd managed to deny it until then, not only for the ten months since I'd announced to Robert that I needed to move on, but also for the months, perhaps years, preceding that point. Now I had to face who I'd become while leaving my marriage and then pretending to myself that it wasn't really over. It hadn't been to "find myself" that I'd left Robert the previous autumn, as was the cliché then (and maybe still is among those who are, even now, finding it necessary to rearrange the relational patterns of their lives). I'd felt quite acquainted with myself, thank you, for as long as I could remember. It was that I believed—and still know I was right to believe despite the difficulty in making it reality—that I could be a good parent only if I weren't trying to ward off someone else's expectations about what a mother should be.

Of course it was more complicated than that, and harder to explain, but there was something about the way Robert began calling me "Mommy" after Mike and Brenda were born that had lodged in my chest and refused to budge until I addressed it. I suppose there was something about my own oedipal issues, or whatever it is that the oedipal complex is a metaphor for, that I simply could not reconcile with Robert's way of working out his issues in relation to me as the mother of his children. But this is digression from the simple point that on the first of July during the summer before my thirty-fourth birthday, I knew the meaning of loneliness in a way I'd not encountered it before.

ON A MILD SUMMER evening two days later I sat on the front bumper of my late-model Buick sipping a glass of merlot after the scene with Robert. On the wide asphalt of our duplex apartment's driveway I watched my children learning to roller blade.

"Hey, girl," I heard behind me, and turned to see Rebecca, my neighbor from the duplex next door, making her way through the bushes between our properties.

"Hey," I said. "How's it going?"

"Alright, but guess what! I'm moving!"

"Moving! How so?" I kept one eye on Mike, who was chasing Brenda around my other neighbor's red Tempo. "Hey! Be careful you guys!" I noticed, with some satisfaction, that my words brought an immediate effect. Brenda took a wider arc around the sedan as Mike pulled himself up short, bending over to rest his hands against his knees as he took a breather and let his sister gain some lead.

Rebecca sat down beside me on my bumper. She opened a wine cooler that she'd brought with her.

"You know that won't last, don't you?" she said, taking a swig.

"What? Their listening to me?"

"Exactly! How old are they now—seven and nine?"

"Yep—seven and nine."

"Great kids! But wait about five years!"

"I know! I know!" I laughed. I'd been told enough times how hard it was parenting teenagers. Now in her early fifties, Rebecca was enjoying the fact that she'd made it through her own children's adolescence with only a few catastrophes—nothing fatal, she had assured me more than once over a cup of tea or glass of wine, but pretty bad at the time. Bad enough that she hadn't been sure she'd make it without bailing one of them out of jail or, worse, supporting a drug-impaired offspring into adulthood. As it turned out, one of her sons was now a graduate student at Northwestern—in theater I think—and the other was refinishing sailboats with his now-sober father in the Keys. Her daughter had apparently come out okay too. But I needed to concentrate on the here and now. That was challenge enough, and all I could hope was that I'd have the resources to cross whatever bridges I came to down the road.

"You're doing a great job with them, Ollie," she said gently. Rebecca was the only friend I had besides Robert who called me Ollie.

"Thanks." I meant it. She met my gaze with her kind blue eyes for a moment before looking away.

"So what's this about moving?"

"Yours truly was offered a job today!"

"Yeah? Which one?"

"Research librarian at the University of Michigan!"

"Oooh, girl!" My delight was only half put on. We clinked our drinks. "The job you interviewed for last year! Great going!"

"Thanks." The pride showed in her face. "They must've liked my presentation. I think they were just waiting for funding."

"Of course they liked you! So when does it start?"

"Well, that's the catch. They need me now." I almost laughed at the face she made, scrunching her forehead comically as she lifted a freckled hand to scratch that curly brown hair.

"I've got to talk to Lucas tomorrow about my lease. I hope he'll let me out of it. But either way," she said, finishing her drink with a final flourish," "I've got to go!"

"And when you've got to go . . ."

"You've got to go!" We finished the phrase together and laughed. I wasn't feeling lonely now, I suddenly realized. At the same moment, I understood how much of a loss Rebecca's leaving was. I'd miss my friend and neighbor of the last ten months. When I swallowed the rest of my wine, the tightness had returned to my throat, and the evening seemed quieter. The light had waned a bit. Mike and Brenda now sat on the other side of the Tempo, talking out of my earshot as they gestured with earnest attention to the straps on Mike's roller blades and the laces on Brenda's.

"Listen, Ollie, I've got a favor to ask you."

"Sure, Rebecca. What is it?"

"Do you think you could keep my piano for a while? Just until I can come back and have it transported? It's the only furniture I have worth keeping, and the rest I'm just going to sell or donate."

"Sure, Rebecca," I assured her, my voice drifting into the closing dusk. "No problem."

A few days after the children and I'd returned from my sister's Independence Day celebration in Orlando—naturally without Robert—

the piano arrived at our duplex. Nick Atherton, a very kind and generous—as well as very fit—friend Rebecca knew from the maintenance department at the university, and Harley, Rebecca's neighbor on the other side, carried it over from Rebecca's by-then almost vacant apartment on a pair of dollies.

I worried what Mr. Lucas would say when he saw that they'd cut a small pathway through the ficus hedge between the properties, in order to avoid taking the piano three times as far around the hedge. No one had consulted me about that detail; when I protested, Harley told me that ficus is the fastest growing herb this side of Nashville, so not to worry. But I was partial to Mr. Lucas, who came every month to trim the hedges and weekly to mow the lawn. I was still feeling guilty as I held the screen door as far as it could open while Rebecca called instructions from inside: "A little to the left—oops! Don't dent the doorjamb!" Nick and Harley maneuvered the instrument onto its side. Somehow—don't ask me how—it fit.

I can make sense of what happened next only by remembering how hot it was that July morning in Delray, and how heartbroken I was knowing I was truly divorced ten months after the actual legal event. I was a thirty-three-year-old mother without even a boyfriend to hold my edges together at night. As Nick brought the piano with a grunt over the threshold into the living room, I saw the sweat running in narrow, sunburned creases down his neck. Through the screen I could also smell his slightly musky perspiration. My own skin began to feel different as I watched him.

I followed Nick into the room. It had been at least two weeks since I'd last seen Robert. I told myself I needn't beat up on myself for lusting after a strong, cute man with a sweet musky smell and a physique as generous and as muscular as his disposition and his biceps, respectively.

"Hey, guys, want a beer?" I offered. It was ten o'clock on a Wednesday morning but nobody seemed to be watching the clock. I wondered if Nick had to get back to work or if he was off today. A wave of fear and excitement ran through me.

"Sure thing, thank you kindly." Nick nodded, as he and Harley pushed the piano against the wall where I'd made a clearing between the television on its shaky stand and the baker's rack I used as bookshelf.

"Yes, ma'am, don't mind if I do," Harley said and winked, running his hands backward over his skull as if to slick back a nonexistent head of hair. Harley never seemed to feel self-conscious about his early balding or the long birthmark that ran the length of his neck from his left ear to the neck of his muscle shirt. He looked older than his thirty or thirty-one years. He was a good guy.

"You want one too, Rebecca?" I extended a long-necked bottle toward her. When I handed Harley and Nick theirs, Nick winked. He'd obviously felt my flirtatious vibes and had no objection. He smiled as he took a long drought. I knew he knew he was in.

BY TWO IN THE afternoon I sat on the new-to-me piano bench, staring at the closed lid over the keyboard and wondering if the kids, when I picked them up from camp, would be able to see that I'd been crying. I had two hours to recover. I ran my finger along the hinge and mentally retraced the morning's events.

Everything had fallen into place when Rebecca left. "Want to come with us?" Harley asked as they were loading her stuff into the trunk of the Chevy he'd already bought from her (and was using to drive her to the airport) while I stood fighting my useless and silly tears in the driveway.

"Better not," Rebecca answered before I even took a breath. She winked, but I saw her struggling as well. "Ollie and I might make a scene and cry all through the airport. Besides," she added, throwing the briefcase she'd d bought for her interview last year into the back seat, "I think she has some things to do here." It occurred to me she was hiding behind a savvy she didn't feel.

"All right," Harley accepted. "I guess we'll be off. Olivia, if Mr. Lucas comes around, tell him that ficus will fill in fast."

As I hugged Rebecca goodbye (making her promise to call me when she'd settled into the furnished apartment already set up for her), I knew Nick was purposely dawdling, waiting until the coast was clear. I was losing a best-friend neighbor within a week of losing an ex-husband. Still, I could feel a spark of the forbidden overtaking my sense of foreboding.

Nick said his goodbyes quickly and climbed in his white pickup, sending me a quick accomplice's glance as he opened the driver's side door. We all waved, and he drove along just ahead of the others, but I had a pretty good hunch he'd be back before the Chevy was out of sight.

He was. When the doorbell rang, I was changing into my swimming suit—the next best thing to sexy underwear, I figured, and more practical since I knew we'd need to rinse off the morning's sweat. What better way than in the semi-private pool behind the duplex, shared only with one set of neighbors who worked during the day?

I answered the door. There he was, grinning a little, and moving in as fast as I was moving toward trouble myself.

"Going swimming?" he asked me, I think a little surprised at my attire.

"It's hot," I said.

He was hot too, he said. I agreed. I hoped he wouldn't mind swimming nude. It was safe, I assured him, since the hedge was protection, and we certainly would need protection. Yes, he always made sure he had protection. With that settled, I led him through my kitchen out the Florida room door to the pool. We didn't swim long.

He didn't stay long, either, afterward. I supposed that was a good thing. His quick exit gave me some time to begin recovering from the surprise I'd given myself, and from Rebecca's departure.

So THERE I SAT at two o'clock on a Monday afternoon in July, having in one morning already made waffles for three, packed two kids off to summer day camp, directed the move of a piano, become complicit in the abuse of a ficus hedge, said goodbye to a friend for what felt like forever (except that she had left something quite tangible behind for which she promised to return), seduced a man I'd never met before in my life, and sent him packing. Of course the last bit was true only in a poetic sense, since Nick had really sent himself packing.

I'd played it ultra-cool as he dressed. "I have a lot to do today," I informed him.

"Me too," he said and made a point of looking at his watch and being surprised that the afternoon was upon us.

"Excuse me just a few minutes," I said, intending to dress out of sight in the bathroom. But he said he'd better just be going right away, and, barely leaving a second between the fastening of his belt and the tousling of my hair that I'm sure he intended as a gesture of endearment, or at least of appreciation, made ready to hit the door.

I wrapped myself in the Ninja Turtle beach towel that I'd used to dry off from the pool. "Thanks for helping out today!" I chirped.

He caught the drift and grinned. "Happy to be of service, ma'am." He was cute. He gave a kind of peace-sign salute as he slipped out the door.

I put my wet swimsuit back on and hit the pool. I swam fast, making quick laps. The sun beat down ferociously, and I was glad. I stayed under the water for as long as possible, doing what I liked to think of as the dead woman float until I'd achieved a seriously altered state. It was amazing to notice the colors of my own hands, floating as if lifelessly before me, and to look down at my red-painted toenails as if they were not connected to me at all. My hair looked like seaweed, floating in a wide swaying arc around my suspended head. A spot right between my shoulders felt as hot as the sand at midday the beach. I tried to convince myself that everything was cool.

Eventually I wrapped the Ninja Turtle towel around me again and walked in a stupor back into the house. I changed into clothes, and then I sat down at the piano. I pushed back the lid and carefully pressed a key, as if afraid it might actually make a sound. It didn't. Then I struck for real. Middle C. A voice from the past told me to find the two black keys together, then slide down to the white key to the left of the pair, and that is middle C.

I played haltingly at first. Then, my heart took a little leap. I felt a stab of nostalgic pleasure as I watched my hand play the right-hand part of "The Entertainer." I tried it with both hands, making it through the first verse and repeating but with a different ending the second time. I was rusty, but I was surprised at how much I did remember. I couldn't recall how it went from there, so I played "Heart and Soul" the way I'd taught myself as a child: my right hand playing the top hand melody and my left bouncing between octaves to play the accompanying call-and-echo chord progression. I was starting to feel better. In fact, I was starting to feel something I'd not felt for longer than I could really remember, and, although I wasn't sure what it was, I can look back and say that it was hope.

I KEPT ON FOR quite a while, scraping around in my memory for whatever my fingers used to know how to play: pieces of Beatles songs—"Hey Jude" through the part about making it better by letting it under your skin, a bit of "The Long and Winding Road," and a fair portion of "Let it Be." It must have sounded atrocious to anyone who might have happened to be listening. If I'd worried about that, though, I doubt that I'd even have cared, which for me is saying a lot.

Just as I was losing some of the steam I'd been riding on, the doorbell rang. For a split second, I believed it was Nick coming to express second thoughts about leaving so quickly. After my escape from self-absorption for the last forty-five minutes, I kicked myself for even considering that anything Nick had to say to me at this point could possibly matter. I needn't have, though, for it was Mr. Lucas, the landlord. He stood at the open door peering disappointedly at me above his glasses, a lock of gray hair almost covering one lens. As always, he wore a denim long-sleeved shirt, jeans, and work boots, even though this was July in Florida.

"Olivia?" he asked, as if he thought it might possibly be someone else in Olivia's body opening the door. "Did you see the hedge?"

I knew he wouldn't believe I'd had anything to do with the large cut-away through the middle of the hedge between his properties. I was an ideal tenant, in his eyes; I knew he felt this way not only because I truly had been, but also because he'd often told me so. "Oh, Mr. Lucas," I said in the manner of one consoling a robbery victim. "It's terrible, I know."

"What could have happened to it?" he asked in a way that nearly made me laugh, shaking his head and opening his palms. "It looks as if it were done deliberate!"

I put my hand on his shoulder, both as a gesture of comfort and to guide him away from the door as I stepped outside and closed the door behind me. "Let's go look," I suggested. When we stood in front of the hole in the hedge, I explained what had happened. To my surprise, I also told him that I felt as if I were a ficus hedge myself and that someone had cut a hole through me—that my ex had found someone new and was no longer considering a reconciliation with me and the children. Worse yet, I told him, as he well knew since he was her landlord, Rebecca—who'd become a very close friend—was gone. He put his arm around me, and there we stood, a sixty-seven-year-old landlord and a woman the age of his youngest daughter, standing in one apartment parking lot looking at another through a piano-sized hole in a ficus hedge.

The midday heat emanated off the black pavement when the kids and I returned home after I'd picked them up from camp. I could feel it under my sandals, seeping into the bottoms of my feet and creeping up my ankle bones. The phone was ringing inside the duplex. Let it ring, I decided as I reached the door, a little surprised at this uncharacteristic splash of nonchalance. Normally I was still as much a sap over a ringing phone as I'd been in my adolescence, eager to know who might be calling to rescue me from mundanity and boredom. I wasn't bored now, I realized. Later, when Mike's excitement over the piano had waned, and Brenda's was beginning to wax, I sat on the couch contemplating the strange and taxing day I'd spent. Something was different, and it wasn't a bad kind of different, though I couldn't quite put my finger of the difference itself.

"Mom," Mike said, settling himself into a seated position under my feet just as I stretched out on the couch. "What does it mean to be on the rag?"

Some things, I guessed, would never change.

A LOT DID CHANGE that summer though, starting with that day. I resolved to have days like today more often. Well, maybe not *quite* like today, but it would be nice, I thought, to feel this much back in touch with myself on a regular basis. I told the kids they could have anything they wanted for dinner. Mike gave Brenda a look. She shrugged as if to say *go figure!* Pizza!" she shouted.

"Pizza and pineapple!" shouted Mike.

"And ice cream!" Brenda added.

"Okay. I'll order the pizza and you two stick a can of pineapple in the freezer."

I vowed then to make our dinners more festive on a regular basis. For ice cream, we went to Doc's, where we finished our cones amid a colorful and rather loud group of fellow customers. At the far end of the patio, two slightly intoxicated young men struck confident poses, overseeing the territory as they waited for their order.

The next morning I woke before dawn to a sense of anticipation before I could place its source. Then I remembered the piano. It seemed funny that a musical instrument in the house could have this effect, but what the hell—I could live with this, and much more easily than I could live with the cloud of depression I realized I'd been under. I got up, and, out of curiosity, decided to check inside the bench. What I discovered was a yellow, well-thumbed book of exercises and arrangements by Clemente. The tattered cover seemed like an old friend. My own copy, long lost, had once been a well-used companion.

I felt a comforting sense of order slipping into place as I flipped through the book and I followed the notes silently with my eyes. They were just black dots on a page, but they were also so much more. Nameless sonatinas, one after the other, filled fifty or sixty pages from top to bottom along horizontal black lines. In the fuzzy silence of the awakening day my body breathed in time with the rhythm I could sense, rather than hear. It was as if I were fourteen years old again, when I'd looked forward my life laid out before me. The chaos of the household in which I'd lived then always receded to the background when I played, tamed into order by the one element that made sense— the logical order of black notes along those black lines.

Standing next to Rebecca's piano these nineteen years later, I played the notes in my head—the top line, then the bottom, then both together. I could nearly hear the music. I didn't want to actually play yet for fear of waking up the kids, but I could pretend to play. That sane, structured arrangement called my fingers to the keys, and I gently applied the pattern I saw before me on the page to the softly depressing keys. Their smooth, cool surfaces yielded silently to my eager and yet self-controlled fingers.

WHEN ROBERT CALLED ONE morning a week or so later—unexpectedly since it wasn't his day to pick up the kids—I noticed a difference in my reaction. Whether I was projecting a desired outcome or finding in myself an actual strength, I attributed it to the fact I'd spent part of every day that that week at the piano, carving out of soft ivory a world I preferred.

"I'm in a bind, Ollie," he said. Was he using my nickname to try to ingratiate me?

"Are you?" I'd answered the corded phone in the kitchen and immediately felt tethered. "Give me a second." I put the phone against the Mexican tile on the counter that Mr. Lucas had put in the previous

Christmas for me. Maybe Robert wanted to switch his weekend schedule with the kids so he could get away with Cindy, his new girlfriend.

"I'm back," I said, picking up the cordless phone from its cradle beside the bed, where Brenda still lay curled in my blue checkered sheets. Her pajamas blended into their pattern like a pinwheel on a hand-stitched quilt. Sweet girl. Her hair cascaded over her face making her look like Cousin It from the old *Addams Family* reruns.

"Ollie, listen," Robert said. "This may sound strange, but could I come over and see you and the kids all together today? I just—I just need to see my family."

Oh boy, I thought, here we go.

I walked through the back screen porch to the pool area, immediately feeling the sun on my face, and lowered myself to the side of the pool. I kicked the surface of the cool water gently with one foot, pulling the other foot against my bum to make a chinrest of my knee, which I hugged to me tightly for support.

Around the edges of the pool were the same Mexican tiles Mr. Lucas had put in the kitchen. Against the back wall of the duplex leaned our pink and green blow-up raft. One side of my mind played with the image of that raft over the conversation that followed, transforming it into a giant telephone that floated, bobbing a bit at the end of a coiled rope, in the middle of the pool.

"We're not exactly your family, Robert. Had you forgotten that, or did you just want to take a break from reality today?"

"Don't be that way, Olivia." His voice was doing that attractive thing. Damn. "I've been thinking about what you said."

"What might I have said, I wonder?" I said, as if in aside. The raft bobbed in my mind's eye.

"Let's all go down to the pier for lunch like we used to, what d'ya say?" He knew my soft spots, and our old tradition was one of them—bacon and eggs at the café across from the beach on a Saturday morning, then a long walk watching the fishermen on the pier as we sipped iced coffee from paper cups and let our food settle before changing into our suits in the pier bathrooms and taking the children into the waves.

"I'm sorry, Robert. I can't do that again."

"Do what?"

I STOOD UP, RAISING my eyes to the line of royal palms that reached from the lot's edge toward the sky. A blue expanse, exactly the color of the sky-blue crayon that had been my favorite as a child, stretched above me with only a few wispy strands of white clouds hovering above the treetops. Pretty.

"Olivia?"

"I'm here."

"What can't you do?"

There was no way to reason with Robert; he was stuck in the same cycle that I had been for so long. It wasn't a matter of him, or of me. It was both of us. With the warmth of the still-early day massaging my skin, I saw clearly that we were complementary elements in a perpetual dance of flight, attraction, and confrontation. The simple solution was to change the tune, or to do a different dance to a different tune. All my self-help reading and two years of intermittent therapy hadn't been for naught. This was, however, the first time I knew myself to be consciously, and conscientiously, applying the principles of helping oneself to help oneself. There was a kind of musical logic in in this newfound, or newly rediscovered, ability.

"Robert, maybe I misspoke. I *could* do what you're asking. But I don't choose to. "

"You don't CHOOSE to! What kind of soft-boiled pop-psychology rhetoric is that?"

His emphasis on the word "choose" reminded me of a Melville's Bartleby, and I almost laughed. I pictured myself stubbornly backed up against an office cubicle at school, my arms crossed across my chest, repeating over and over, "I'd prefer not to." I felt some compassion, but for some reason—most likely to lighten the situation by retreating to irony—I repeated the phrase.

For a moment the only sound was our breathing. His was rather fast and uncomfortable sounding, but I felt as if mine were flowing into the air like the wispy clouds now dissipating into the clear blue sky.

"Listen, Robert," I continued, "I don't want to put ourselves through this off-and-on again business anymore. And I—

"We can fix that."

"I don't want to fix it."

"How can you not want to fix it?"

"Robert, will you listen to me?"

Again, only silence. Then I told him how I thought we'd both been trying to hold on, often at different times, to something that hadn't for one reason or another been working for a long time. That it didn't even matter who it was that had been holding on at any particular time; we kind of depended on each other. "We know that when at least one of us is doing the holding on, the other can keep us from getting too intimate by resisting." I took a breath. Robert still seemed to be holding his. "It's true symbiosis," I continued. "I think that's the right word—and we're so tied into our symbiotic pattern that we don't even know we're doing it." There was still no sound on the other end. "I'm tired, Robert. I want to move on."

Of course, I insisted, I cared about him, and of course it had been hard, and I was sure it would still be hard, but I had to do this. "Or I really should still say I choose to do this. I'm not going back anymore." He could still see the kids, and I'd never say anything bad about him to them, and I hoped he'd do the same for me, and we'd follow our agreement and raise them jointly. But we would do so separately and apart from any relationship per se between us except in relation to them. I hoped he'd respect my decision. I hoped he'd understand.

"Blah, blah, blah," he said. I was surprised at his response, though I might not have been. At first, I felt angry, but I decided not to respond in the way that had become, through practice and habit, most familiar.

"Okay," I said. "So do you want to pick up the kids today?"

"Blah, blah, blah."

"I'll tell you what," I decided. "I'm going to hang up now. You can see the kids if you want, as long as you let me know by eleven. You can leave a message on my machine. We're going out to do some errands, but we'll be home by about three, and you can pick them up then if you like. Okay?"

There was no response, so I softly hit the "off" button on the cordless and went back inside. Mike was in front of the television already, eating a bowl of raisin bran, so engrossed in the exploits of the *Gargoyles* as I passed through his line of vision that he didn't notice me, even when I bent down to hug him and give him a kiss on the top of the head.

The bedroom opened off the living room, so it was just a few steps from Mike to Brenda, who was only beginning to stir in the too-big bed. I lay down beside her and cuddled her to me as she sighed and snuggled into me. "Time to get up now, baby."

"Okay, Mommy," she said, her eyes still closed.

I AWOKE SOME TIME later to see Mike standing above me, one foot planted firmly on the dresser under the window, the other propped against the bed about a foot from my head as he adjusted the Venetian blinds. Sunlight poured over us like crystal sugar from a feed sack. I looked up, squinting into the cloud of light in which stood my son, looking like a sweet but somewhat annoyed angel. His hair was all illuminated, and his face nearly obscured by the brightness around him.

"What's up, sweetie?" I asked sleepily.

"Just me!"

I sat up, laughing. Brenda stirred next to me. I jostled her, filled with an unmistakable sense that all was right with the picture. 'Time to get up, baby." Hadn't I said that an hour ago?

Mike jumped to the floor and stood with his arms akimbo. "Dad called."

HOURS LATER, WE WERE laughing when we went into the living room to see Robert at my door with Cindy. I'd never met her, but I knew right away that's who it was. She stood a bit nervously behind Robert, extending her hand to Mike to whom she had apparently just been introduced.

Robert smiled as if confronted with an unexpected meeting with someone very insignificant in his life but to whom, especially because he must show some manners in front of his children, he had to be courteous.

"Mom," said Mike, turning to look over his shoulder at me, "this is Cindy." His expression indicated he wasn't sure how I'd respond. My chest tightened a bit with a pang of sympathy for him. I decided to respond kindly.

"Hey, Cindy." Cindy straightened up from the shy and timid posture she had taken with Mike and became a woman protecting her rights. Her handshake was firm.

"Glad to meet you," she said, looking me straight in the eye as if there were some contest going on.

No way was I interested in competing for Robert. Maybe I had, in a sense, been competing for his attention, competing for a place on his priority list with my own silly dance of intimacy and avoidance the last ten months. But there was absolutely no way under the Florida sun I would play this game, not on my own turf nor anywhere else. I had a very strong urge to play the piano. That's what I did, as soon as they were safely out the door. And that's what I did again and again throughout that increasingly less painful summer.

BY THE END OF August, I'd steadily improved my keyboard skills through careful and patient practice. I was no virtuoso at the keys and am not to this day, but between the lines of Mozart's "Sonata K. 545" and

Clemente's "Rondo-Valse," I did find a part of myself that had been hiding for several years. In Beethoven's "Bagatelle, Op. 126, No. 5" I took a few chances (less risky and more rewarding than sexual flirtations of the kind I'd engaged in with Nick). And in the easy and eventually intermediate-level arrangements of Beatles music, I took comfort and found a kind of relief and release. I understood what I'd read about cultivating a craft or an art as what Robert Frost called a stay against confusion. I realize now I was cultivating not only a craft or an art, but a real refuge from suffering.

The therapist I'd been seeing through the employee assistance program at work told me I was engaging in neurological reprogramming. When I explained how I'd resisted lashing out at or succumbing to Robert' pleadings when, in the wee hours of the morning on a mid-August night, he appeared at my door drunk and demanded entrance, she told me I was indeed regrooving old patterns of behavior by creating new ones.

Twice that month, once before and once after the drunkenness incident, I had, out of incredible loneliness and desperation for human companionship (beyond that of my children or work colleagues, or just plain horniness), dialed his number, determined to ask him over. But both times I'd come to my senses, once before the phone had actually rung, the other before I'd said anything that would send us back into a spinning pool of confusion. My therapist took my newfound strength as further evidence that I was on a healing course. After the eight sessions allotted to me through the EAP, we decided the therapy had been successful.

ONE AFTERNOON THAT SEPTEMBER as my little family was arriving home from school, Rebecca called. She was sorry she hadn't phoned sooner—she'd been so busy. I'd missed her too—the job was going well—the kids were good. She was ready to retrieve her piano.

I STAYED UP LATE that night going over my checkbook. Was there any way to buy a replacement for the instrument that had meant so much to me the past few weeks? Did I really need it? I fell asleep that night without turning off the kitchen light, as if I were afraid of the darkness that lay with sense of impending loss just around the corner.

When I awoke in earnest, the sky outside my window was beginning to lighten. I pulled Robert's old robe over the tank top and shorts I'd slept in, opened the duplex's front door, and stepped into the parking lot. Closing the door quietly, I surveyed the quiet neighborhood. The strip of our duplex apartments is the top crossbar of a T, of which my front door forms the connecting point. A long residential street flanked with single family homes extends eastward. Beyond it, a mile or so away, lies the ocean.

As I stood there that early morning I had the impression, even in this flattest of landscapes, that I was at the top of a hill looking downward over a kingdom. Above the tree line where my T fades into the horizon, the pink expanse of sky was becoming lighter. Dawn rolled off the ocean, making its way over the line of sea grapes and condos at the shoreline, crossing inland a short distance to reach us.

Nearby a single engine started and wound into gear as some early riser made way to a job. Otherwise, all was silent. The morning paper lay next to that perpetually evaporating puddle near the end of the parking lot. I ventured across the pavement to retrieve it. The Ixora next to my mailbox displayed their tight clusters of pink blossoms. Tidy pebbles adhered themselves to the palms of my feet. On my way back to the door with the paper, I saw that the ficus hedge where Nick and Harley had made an opening for Rebecca's piano was entirely filled in. I knew I'd somehow afford a new piano.

AND I DID. NOT long afterward, I found in the classified ads a notice from a music store offering financing for pre-owned instruments with only 20 percent down. I called; the only piano in my price range was an electronic keyboard. "It plays and sounds like a piano," the saleswoman assured me. "And it has the full eighty-eight keys."

With something between disappointment and excitement I drove to the Pompano Beach store after teaching my two sections of Freshman Comp II (and packing into my bag another fifty-three papers to be graded on the topic of why so-and-so is a dynamic character). Within two hours I backed the Buick into the duplex parking lot with the Rhodes '88 extending out of the trunk, secured with bungee cords and wrapped in two shipping blankets I'd promised to return to the music store.

It sat next to Rebecca's piano until she came to retrieve it the next weekend. I picked her up at the airport in West Palm Beach on Friday night and brought her home. We stayed up laughing and talking into the early hours. The next day, Harley and a friend of his—to my relief it wasn't Nick—loaded the piano into the U-Haul truck that she'd rented for the drive back to Michigan, and away went my two dear friends, Rebecca and her piano.

A LOT HAS HAPPENED in the three years since that summer. Mike is now in middle school, nearly as tall as I am, and in training to play football this season, despite my protests—mild since he is my son—that the sport is a form of war games. Brenda is taking piano lessons and practices on the Rhodes, sometimes with the headphones until she is satisfied, then proudly unplugging them to perform for us a newly acquired piece in her repertoire.

I love the headphones myself, for many a night when the kids are in bed I will play myself out of the tensions of the day at the little keyboard that sounds and feels almost like a real piano. There's nothing like the quiet that settles over the apartment and the neighborhood around midnight. I'll often step outside after playing and breathe in the salty air that drifts inland from the ocean. Although I can't hear it from here, I take comfort in knowing that ocean is there, steadily keeping its rhythm against the world's changes.

On the weekends that Brenda and Mike stay over at Robert and Cindy's house, I use the headphones so I don't wake my new lover.

Charles tends to fall asleep after we have merged, body and soul, in the kind of sex I had thought at one point I was incapable of experiencing with anyone after Robert. At such times I find myself infused with life and ready to embrace the world and all its opportunities. Charles is a sweetie, a real gentleman, and I don't mind that he falls asleep before I do. I just listen for the regularity of his breath, the deep repose of his chest muscles beneath my head. Then I extract myself carefully from his arms, kiss him softly on his slightly open mouth, and make my way silently to the Rhodes. With my headphones on, I can't even hear him snoring. But I can see my fingers leaping and dancing as they send those sweet, staccato, or soothing tones through the digital sensors inside the keyboard. Sometimes I have to remind myself that those are really my hands doing that, that those are really my fingers dancing there, transforming my conscious patterns of movement and reaction—of love and fear and neurosis and joy—into the music that I hear.

Provisioning Between Lives

Joanne Gram

Piloting my existential ship once more
to the all essentials superstore
to pick up some special supplies

Bitch CD playing
soul talking
She knows what she wants
what she can afford for sure
Maybe I do too

Pull up to the automatic door
Cart has a funky wheel
but I kick the plastic crud chunks
off my edges and we're shopping
rolling to old time market music

Organic red raspberries cost
same as the rest
just different currency
Best to save a bit of Earth
Worth remembering
never to live fruitlessly

Bakery aura of hot glaze and yeast
Gotta be sweet and rising
I take at least enough for me

plus some to share if someone dares
my appetizing bakery surprises

Double back for ears of corn
Steamy, buttery, salty
that's me
A side dish or maybe a whole meal
if I feel like it, and I do feel like it
But keep those tassels out of my eyes
because they make me cry
Little things can still make me cry

Red meat, whitefish
Red wine, white wine
Some balancing act of
protein and spiritual strength
Vodka with a name
I can't pronounce but
not Russian this time
Back to produce for
lemons and limes

Taking time
checking the floral section
A selection of markdown plants
I will work to revive
To transplant and thrive in
my next situation.

Proper treats, toys, and
temper for pets I will acquire
It pays to be a careful buyer
for keeping any living creatures
happy and healthy

Up and down every aisle with
the patience of sharp aging cheese
Building upon a growing essence
requires a certain presence of mind
A new life must not leave behind
necessary items or savory tidbits

Smiling I roll my bulging cart
back to the start by the opening door
Pleased with the mixture of
sweet with tart
fresh and properly preserved
Fill environmentally friendly
bags with those cute earthy graphics
Self-check out
paying the total
Carefully load everything
into my vessel

Setting a course back into traffic
Greeting the moving world again
Watching out for first time drivers
Singing along with
an old smooth song by Holly Near
Something about love

I taste the raspberries

Happy Birthdays to Me!

J. Michele Moll

With trembling hands, richly laced with fine blue veins, I open the gifts
of "old"
and marvel at the shiny, sparkling possibilities, long-kept secrets
unfolding as
I celebrate 60 years on this earth
So many precious, lovely gifts of age, the glory and the promise of
more olding
The surprising, soft sweetness of sagging skin, the wonderous warmth
of wattles, the lure of luxurious lumps, the magnificence of my lover's
man muscles and his lion liver beneath his soft papery skin.
Finally free of the tyrannical trap of youthful, physical beauty—
bursting like so many bright balloons
Filled with the strange and terrible expectations of strangers
Mouth-watering presents promised to me, but never surely mine until
my oldness made it so,
Holding these close now in my lined and unsure hands, close to my
withered and satisfied breast

I am free to dance at my party, with unsteady gait, finding my sure
footing in found truths and the joyous lightness of gnarled toes,
sweetly calloused soles, trembling limbs
Tattooed with each small fluttery kiss, every time our foreheads met,
the touch of a warm hand tracing the graceful arc of my spine curling

over the laughter lovingly gathered in my lapping at the dew of yet
another sweet morning, the joyous savory tiered confection of so
many years
Warm and fragrant from the kiln, baked through with the knowledge
that what is—is enough,
Has always been enough,
Yet more is to come. How am I so blessed?

I catch my breath.
Such a lovely party!
No one ever told me it would be like this

Every year the gift of another candle so that—all lit now—the world is
gloriously aflame,
Mind-blowingly aglow, shining from within and without, lighting the
ways and wealth of wild wishes
Banishing the dark sweaty fears and muskily redolent anxieties of
youth like so many bad dreams
Knives are lost and dull, cruel truths are dusty pictures in a shoebox on
the closet shelf
Ice cream colors of my choices running together promising more
honeyed happenings
I taste the sweet confection of my many days lingering on the tongue,
summoning more,
I hear the joyous song erupt in a tremulous voice, hopeful and finally
and happily old
This sweet, sweet song of old, old, olding life

Happy, happy, happy birthdays to me!

The Protector

Margaret Speck Ogawa

THE MOON HUNG IN THE INKY SKY, LACED BY GHOST-LIKE CLOUDS. IT WAS CLOSE to midnight. Outside, a howling wind threw itself against my brick home. I listened briefly as the windows rattled, then continued with my pleasure reading—an indulgence I enjoyed during the undemanding hours while my household slept. Beneath the lashing air, I heard a loud scraping and then a sudden bang. I dropped my book, flew to the window, pressed my forehead against the cold glass, and peered out. Familiar shapes, in shades of black, silhouetted the yard. Clasping my bathrobe together, I flicked on the outdoor lights. Was someone out there? Trying to break into the basement? Would he or *they* be armed? Adrenaline coursed as my ears pulsed and crime scene photos from *In Cold Blood* and the Manson murders flashed in my head.

What to do? I quickly evaluated. It was probably nothing, not worth waking the husband or calling the police, and yet—it could be *something*. Something dangerous. Something threatening. Something that could enter my home and harm my children sleeping peacefully in their footed pajamas. NOT AT MY HOUSE!

I'd developed the practice of tackling problems head-on during my formative years belting out the hit song "I Am Woman." It was my anthem. When I sang it, I believed it. The lyrics' message of invincibility and strength gave me not only the confidence to "roar" (don't mess with me, baby), but the song and the whole Women's Lib movement that was front and center during my teen years convinced me it was how I should live my life. I could do anything, Helen Reddy told me. It's funny how a song can enable a young girl into believing so strongly, perhaps sometimes blindly or naively, in the magic of her potential. Thus armed, I felt empowered to face down threats, lurking evils, and bad guys.

When I stepped out the door, frigid air slapped me, but I maintained a ninja-nimble readiness. My eyes nervously raked the side yard. And then I saw, on its side, our plastic, green garbage bin. Ohhh. As I grabbed the can to right it, a creature appeared too close to my feet.

A raccoon! Scruffy and ugly—not cute like Meeko. Dirt clung to its guard hairs, and it issued a feral hiss through bared teeth.

I screamed. With thoughts of rabies flooding my brain—I'd never recovered from *Old Yeller*—I shook my arms and yelled, "Go away, you damn raccoon." As it disappeared down the alley, I released a shaky breath.

My kids loved the *naughty* raccoon story—their own personal family fairy tale. Especially my oldest, Malia. Perhaps it was the line, delivered in my best Arnold Schwarzenegger voice, "because I had to protect my family" that enchanted her and made her feel safe— knowing I was there to protect her. It defined me as the "Protector," kind of like Schwarzenegger's Terminator, and *my* role was reinforced every time she asked me to repeat the family tale. I might even have grown a little conceited about my protective abilities as they took on a kind of superhero status. I loved being my kids' superhero, but, in all honesty, *biology* more than bravery may have provoked my protective response.

Oxytocin, nicknamed the "feel good" or "love" hormone, is believed to cause the bonding between mothers and infants. It also seems to provoke a maternal protective response. When animals perceive danger, they instinctively freeze, or they flee. The Champalimaud Centre for the Unknown, in Lisbon, Portugal, conducted research on oxytocin's influence on protective behavior and the flee instinct. In the study, the presence of oxytocin in mama rats stifled their freeze or flee response when the mamas were threatened while their offspring were present—thus risking potential harm to protect their babies. When the scientists blocked the oxytocin in the mothers' brains, the mama rats neglected their protective duties and merely froze when "danger" appeared. The study's lead scientist concluded that "similar mechanisms may be at play" in humans.

While this study backs up my "biology versus bravery" theory, I found stunning, new research that possibly explains why protective instinct may linger longer in some than others. According to "The New Science of Motherhood" by Abigail Tucker (*Smithsonian Magazine*, (May 2021), scientists have discovered that fetal cells can remain in a mother's body "forever," colonizing her organs and embedding in her breasts and bone marrow. Imagine that. They've even found fetal cells while autopsying the cadavers of old women. Surrogate mothers have them, too. This phenomenon might explain why oxytocin-induced protective instinct may diminish in some, but stubbornly adhere in others. I suspect fetal cells, from my three children, are scattered throughout my own body prompting my protective instinct to rear its feral head the night of the racoon. It also stoked my protective response when a modern-day Bluebeard courted my daughter, Malia.

ONCE UPON A TIME . . .

. . . in the land of sidewalk bistros, butter, and small dogs on leashes, a young American woman fell in love with a doe-eyed, Parisian man. "Mom, he's perfect for me," Malia said. "We're both Tolkien nerds who love *Lord of the Rings* and Sam and Frodo. You'll like him. He's smart. He's an *engineer*."

Across the miles I imagined Malia, phone to ear, eyes lit, her voluptuous curls flat-ironed into drapes of heavy brown silk. To be young, and in love, and in Paris. How adventurous she was! How brave! I admired her for those qualities and for following her dreams.

The two love birds discussed their futures and flew back and forth on weekends between Madrid, where Jean-Luc worked on a long-term engineering project, and Paris, where Malia, an assistant English teacher residing in the Neuilly-sur-Seine neighborhood, had a lengthy commute to a suburban high school outside the city. I worried about my girl's safety on her long, evening commutes home.

"Don't worry, Mom. This isn't the US. They don't carry guns here. Just knives."

As SUMMER APPROACHED, MALIA informed my husband and me that she planned to pursue her master's degree in history from King's College in London. She'd return to Seattle and save money working over the summer. Jean-Luc would visit in August, and she would begin her program in September. Impressive. My daughter was carving out her future as a global nomad. Growing up in Honolulu, I, too, had dreamed of traveling the world. I'd moved as far as the mainland and earned a master's degree but never lived overseas—just visited a handful of countries. I understood her desire to see the world and experience other cultures, and I applauded her ambitions and ability to make them happen—especially since many of my own dreams were unfulfilled.

Although part of me wondered if her global galloping would take precedence over a career. What would studying European history with a specialty in Napoleon and his soldiers yield? Should I cover her costs and make her adventures so easy to obtain? Dreams should be earned. I was not her magic genie. I'd paid my own way since graduating from college. Attended grad school on student loans, a fellowship, and by living frugally. I began to question whether I was being too indulgent. Shaping children sometimes requires standing back, transforming the support, cheering the struggle—building strength and tenacity for the long run. That summer I swam in indecision: How long would we support her global fancies? Were her travels setting her up for a secure future?

Where would this road take her? In the end, we offered to cover her tuition costs and housing. And we would *loan* her the funds to cover her living expenses.

WHEN JEAN-LUC MISSED his Seattle-bound flight because he had forgotten to take his passport with him to the airport, I sympathized knowing how he must have felt at the check-in counter: disbelief, disappointment, embarrassment. Possibly anger. Malia, who'd been so excited to see him, spoke gently with him on the phone, but after the call, misery sat plainly on her face. My daughter has the kind of cheeks you want to cup in your hands. Full and soft and round. I wanted to somehow smooth her sadness away but attempted practicality by focusing on the details of his next flight. He missed that one, too, because he overslept. I can see the brilliant red flags now. For his third attempt, he'd set multiple alarms, and Malia called him to be sure he was up and that his passport was in his carry-on bag. Jean-Luc arrived the second week of August 2015 for an intended three-week stay. With relief, I hugged him and welcomed him to our home.

The first few days, Malia and Jean-Luc were constantly in each other's company, holding hands, touching, sitting close. I smiled at their animated conversations—delighting in their joyful interaction. I love to see couples happily engaged in conversation, and I took this as a good sign.

Malia had scheduled time off work to spend with Jean-Luc, but she was soon back at the hotel spa several days a week. He quickly grew restless and bored and played games on his phone while she was out. Sometimes he rode into Seattle with her and walked around. One afternoon, I asked Jean-Luc to join me while I prepared dinner. He sat at the little table in our kitchen and answered my questions about his engineering job and his life in France. To help him feel like part of the family, I handed him potatoes and a peeler and asked him if he would please help me. When he'd finished the potatoes, he abruptly stood and left the room and did not reappear until I called him for dinner. I regretted asking for his help. Had I had offended him? Did he abhor kitchen work? Or was it something else?

One day I returned home with my arms full of groceries. Malia and Jean-Luc were sipping wine on the patio. Neither stood to help me. As I passed them, I heard Jean-Luc tell Malia, "Yes, she is a bitch," referring to my youngest daughter, Nalani. My baby girl was sixteen years old to his twenty-five. It enraged me, and I began to see shades of misogyny in his language and attitude.

During his second week, Jean Luc declined meals in the house. He would not dine with the family, preferring to eat out of cans he purchased at the grocery store. He smoked pot every day in the gazebo in our front yard. And I heard him disparage Malia's attempts to help Nalani with her French: "Why bother? She'll never get it." As his shy, charming façade crumbled, I silently questioned my daughter's choice and, consequently, her decision-making ability. How far would their romance go? Did she see a future with him? What would that look like? My heart sank as I mentally pulled back my sleeves and steeled for a rough ride.

I tried to think of activities to occupy Jean-Luc while Malia worked, looking forward to his flight home the following week. We talked. He wanted some physical activity, so I pulled out one of my husband's bicycles. Jean-Luc confidently pedaled down the driveway. Elated, I could have turned cartwheels had I been so skilled. But he soon returned. Our neighborhood hills proved too demanding. I found the bicycle discarded on the driveway.

Again, I tried to find something for him to do. His eyes lit up when I suggested that he hit tennis balls with Nalani. I could tell he looked forward to teaching "the bitch" a lesson. I was also pleased because the child was athletically gifted, and the feral raccoon in me wanted to slap the arrogance out of him.

I drove them to an empty neighborhood court, and they began. Jean-Luc shed his mask of indifference fully engaging in the game. His desire to win was clear. Sweat dampened his hair then trickled down the sides of his face. His shirt stuck to his back. Nalani presented friendly politeness as though the match was no big deal, but I knew she wanted to win just as badly as he. The game was close. With a final well-placed shot, Nalani won. I hid my glee, but in a quickly exchanged glance, Nalani and I celebrated the victory. Jean-Luc congratulated her, and we rode home in silence. To Malia, he later blamed the loss on the racket we'd lent him.

Back at the house, he remained alone in the guest room, again skipping dinner with us. Malia arrived home late that night. The next morning, she surprised me by privately expressing joy at Jean-Luc's defeat. She was finding his behavior increasingly annoying, and she told me he'd expected to "beat Nalani's ass." I was delighted with Malia's shared confidence and realized that alliances were shifting. Malia stepping away from Jean-Luc and closer to her family felt almost biblical to me.

In response to Jean-Luc's complaints about boredom, Malia took him to work and treated him to a massage at the spa. After his session, she found him smoking a joint in the men's room and trying to exhale it into the ventilation system. A confrontation followed, and he accused her of having no sympathy for his days spent waiting for her while she worked.

The relationship continued to crack. Malia invited Kate, a ten-year-old girl that she babysat and absolutely adored, to join her and Jean-Luc for a trip to Pike Place Market to browse the produce, crafts, and food stalls and to watch the flying fish. Malia's face was set like stone when they returned. She told me that Jean-Luc had intended to shoplift from one of the small shops they had entered. He'd told Malia that it would be the store owner's fault for making it so easy. Malia's angry response had shut down that idea. She was astounded he would consider shoplifting—especially in Kate's presence.

Her disillusionment was obvious. She told me that he'd confided to her that he'd never worked so hard as he had when he studied to pass his engineering exams, and he never wanted to work that hard again.

And then the pot-growing supplies arrived. Evidently, he'd planned to join her in London and grow weed in her campus apartment and live off its sales. This was Malia's breaking point. He would ruin her life. I thanked God that she had seen the light. Now, like me, and the rest of the family, she was looking forward to his departure for Paris in less than a week's time.

The next day, a knife changed everything. Heightened. Accelerated. Intensified. I feel goose bumps, even now as I tap my keyboard, when I recall the moment I spied Jean-Luc's dagger on the glass-topped table in our guest room. It must have been afternoon. The sun was shining in through the western-facing window. Malia and Jean-Luc had run an errand. Feeling sheepish and intrusive, I entered the room to look about. Malia had told me that morning that Jean-Luc was beginning to frighten her, and that she was going to break up with him. She couldn't wait the four remaining days for his flight home. She would do it today. She confessed that he was taking multiple pills for depression, was smoking weed every day, and was addicted to pain killers.

What?

And that he'd been fired from his job in Madrid and had had a run-in with the Madrid police.

W-h-a-t??? I felt like a wobbling cartoon character with stars spinning around my head.

Okay, I knew about the weed but not about the fantastically shocking rest of it. It was as though Bluebeard's locked door had just sprung open, and I was seeing the rot.

And, she'd continued, Jean-Luc carried a knife for protection.

A knife?

Hadn't I seen him hurling it into the grass, she had asked, in the front yard—practicing accuracy?

About five inches long, its blade glinted in the light. I picked it up feeling the warm, sun-soaked handle in my palm. I pressed my finger to its tip wondering how much pressure I'd have to apply to draw blood. Mine or his. Would he use it against me? Or worse, against Malia or one of my other children? Would Nalani feel its steel penetrate her skin as payback for their humiliating tennis match?

As I reflect on this memory, another knife surfaces. My father-in-law is shaking it threateningly at four-year-old Nalani, angered by something she'd said. The girl had a mouth on her. He'd been living with us for three years and had developed dementia along with his diabetes. My husband traveled frequently, and my stress and agitation had increased as Papa's dementia had slowly progressed.

"You're full of shit!" he spat at me that dreadful evening. Anger filled his voice.

"You're full of shit!" I spat back. "And you're out of here tomorrow." Once the words were out, I couldn't recall them. And I didn't want to. Releasing my pent-up anger felt so good—for a moment. My three kids cowered in the hallway and slept with me in my locked bedroom that night. They were afraid of Papa and afraid he would hurt me. A former boxer, he was still a strong man and an imposing figure. Away in Germany on business, my husband was unable to serve as a buffer. The tension had been building for months. A few weeks earlier, the family had returned to the house to find it filled with gas. Papa had not been able to ignite a flame on the stove and had walked away leaving the burner switched on. He was a good man, but his diabetes and dementia combined to make his presence in our home unsafe for any of us. It was difficult, and the decision carried its share of guilt, but we placed him in a care facility, and then another, and then another, each one better equipped than the previous one to deal with his progressing dementia. He eventually died of heart failure.

The experience of dealing with the danger my father-in-law presented in our home informed my swift reaction to the knife. Jean-Luc had to go.

Malia wasn't strong enough to make him leave. She'd tried. I needed to deliver the message. When I entered the guest room, his packed bag sat on the floor, and he was sprawled stomach down on the bed engaged with his phone. He ignored my presence, but as I watched his averted face, feeling his struggle for dignity, I felt my resolution softening. With a calm voice, I explained that he needed to go back to his home in Paris today. We were going to drive him to the airport—Malia was waiting in the car. He responded that he was looking for a rental car to sleep in until his flight home Sunday. It was Wednesday. I was scheduled to leave town on Friday with my son and husband. I couldn't wait. As long as he was in town, my daughters were at risk. He had to go.

You cannot sleep in a rental car, I told him. He refused to budge. I picked up his packed duffle bag, carried it to my car, and placed it in the trunk. Malia was sitting in the front passenger seat. Jean-Luc eventually exited the house and climbed into the back seat. Halfway to the airport, as he sat behind us, his knife stashed away in his backpack, I realized, too late, the vulnerability of our exposed necks and heads. How stupid I was.

We arrived at the airport heads intact. I dropped Malia and Jean-Luc at the Delta curb and headed to the parking garage. Malia was to purchase Jean-Luc's ticket for an early afternoon flight to Paris. There were plenty of seats: I'd made sure in advance. As I emerged from the garage, Malia called my cell phone. Jean-Luc had run away.

After searching the airport grounds, we drove around the surrounding neighborhood. Useless. He didn't answer Malia's repeated calls to his phone. It threw us into a terrifying limbo of uncertainty. Was he safe? Was he mentally stable? Would he return to the house with his knife? On the one hand, I felt responsible for his safety while in the US. He had come from his mother's home to mine, and although I didn't know her, I felt an affinity as mothers. On the other hand, I couldn't be comfortable with his whereabouts unknown.

At home, Malia and I surveyed the empty guest room. I found a discarded paint-gun box and a gadget for barricading the door closed. The next day, a set of throwing knives arrived for Jean-Luc courtesy of Amazon. I worried he'd return to collect the set once he'd received his delivery notification. I spoke with Amazon's customer service, and they agreed not to send anymore packages to the house for him.

Jean-Luc contacted Malia that evening. He was at an airport motel. They argued. He taunted Malia by suggesting he could drive to the house and stab me or our dog. None of us slept at home that night or the next.

My husband and I left for Wisconsin Friday morning to accompany my son to college. I felt uneasy but determined to continue with our plans. Nalani was spending the weekend with a friend. Malia stayed with my close friends Laurie and Craig, because I didn't want anyone in the house while Jean-Luc lurked about.

At about 1 a.m. in Madison, my phone rang.

"Mom, did you leave the back door open when you left the house?" Malia asked.

I had not. Laurie and Craig had picked her up from a friend's home, and the three had stopped to check on the house. Malia kept me on the phone as they progressed down the hallways and into the rooms, opening doors, checking closets, looking under beds. The background whispers and quiet were unnerving as I flattened the phone to my ear.

"Oh my God, Mom!"

Jean-Luc had thrown a brick through a large window at the top of the stairwell leading to our garage. He had then leaped through the broken window to the bottom landing. Blood and glass littered the carpeted stairs. In Malia's bedroom, they found her bedspread soaked with urine. Jean-Luc later explained, he'd been looking for her and thought she was home but just not answering the doorbell. I still feel sick to my stomach when I picture him entering the house with Malia home alone.

Monday, when we returned from Madison, Malia informed us that Jean-Luc had not returned to Paris on Sunday.

He'd made a friend, Devon, and was staying with this man and his girlfriend. He remained there for several days until Devon's girlfriend kicked him out. His antisocial behavior or his misogyny probably prompted her and her mother to search his belongings. They found his dagger. Well done, girlfriend and girlfriend's mom. Devon took Jean-Luc to a long-stay hotel. From there Jean-Luc called Malia and pleaded for a chance to apologize in person. The idea filled me with dread, but my husband and I agreed to a public meeting with both of us present. At Zeke's Pizza, Jean-Luc and Malia sat in a booth and spoke quietly. He then approached us and apologized for the damage to our home and the havoc he'd caused. Contrite. He used his charming smile to disarm us, and he attributed it all to how crazily in love he was with our daughter. We forgave him. That's not to say we welcomed him back. We took Malia home with us.

The next day, while I shopped for our upcoming trip to London, Jean-Luc arrived at the house with flowers. His time was short. Malia and I were to leave in a few days to settle her in for graduate school. He asked to reconcile. Malia refused. He left the house disappointed and angry. He left her stressed and determined to build a life without him.

WE DRANK COMPLIMENTARY CHAMPAGNE in the lobby, grabbed dinner at Wagamama, then retired to our London hotel room and unpacked. Malia's phone rang. Jean-Luc.

"I don't want to talk to him," she said.

"You have to answer it," I replied.

"Mom, this is making me sick."

"We have to know what's going on, Malia. Where he is."

Malia placed the phone on speaker. "Hello?"

"How could you leave me?" Jean-Luc said. "I'm dying. I'm out of meds. The withdrawal's killing me."

"Where are you?" she asked.

"I'm at a fucking hospital. In the emergency room. They're assholes. I've been waiting for hours. I'm leaving."

"Don't leave. Let them help you."

"It's too late. I've walked out. I have no money. I spent the last of it on weed. Now, I'm just going to live off the land."

"Call Devon."

"I did. He didn't answer. His stripper girlfriend hates me. The whore probably took his phone."

"You can't just live on the street. Call your brother."

"Sébastien's a selfish asshole. He won't help. No one cares."

"I'm worried about you."

"Fuck you. You don't care. You and your family think you are so superior. You're an idiot. Your family are all idiots. You don't care about people."

I regarded my daughter, her face pale, her shoulders hunched.

"I hate you," he said. "You are so selfish. Maybe I will find you in London."

"Hang up," I said.

She did. Within minutes, she'd messaged a mutual Parisian friend of theirs who agreed to contact Jean-Luc's mother. Next, Malia texted Sébastien, the brother who lived in Boston. She then erased Jean-Luc from her life. Blocked. Unfriended. Deleted.

We spent the next few days purchasing necessities for Malia's graduate flat avoiding talk of Jean-Luc. Wanting to raise her spirits, and feeling quite guilty for making her talk to him, I ignored our focus on practical frugality and bought her a brightly painted ceramic teapot with molded figures of Alice, the Mad Hatter, and the Cheshire Cat sprouting from it—vainly hoping it would somehow ease her angst. For not only was she unnerved by Jean-Luc's accusations, hurt by his verbal diatribe, and threatened with a visit, but a small part of her mourned the Tolkien nerd she'd fallen in love with. Worse, he had shaken her confidence in her ability to trust her instincts—for their sweet Tolkien connection had offered her the false promise of safety. She would go on to spend the next year and more suffering from bouts of PTSD, but in the end she would triumph by earning her master's degree in European history and establishing a meaningful relationship with a "worthy" young man from London with whom she currently continues her adventure in Tokyo.

I returned to Seattle, tracked down Jean-Luc, who'd been arrested near the Canadian border for shoplifting, and met with his friend Devon at Jean-Luc's long-stay hotel. There I claimed Jean-Luc's belongings from the room he'd trashed, washed his clothes, and stitched together his ripped canvas travel bag. I unclenched only when I learned of his arrival in Paris escorted by Sébastien.

Then I pulled out my phone and reread Sébastien's last text to me expressing his profound disappointment in my handling of the situation and my treatment of his brother, Jean-Luc. He asked that I give Jean-Luc's bag and clothes to Devon, and emphasized that his family wanted no further contact from me, Malia, or any other family member. The situation no longer concerned me. I'd already done enough.

AUTHOR AND MEMOIRIST ANDRÉ Aciman said, during a small Zoom session on travel writing and memoir, that as people, we do not change. He was responding to a question I'd asked, and I'd had to force my face to remain pleasant. I felt almost insulted by his assertion and wasn't ready to agree. Of course, I've changed. Doesn't personal growth change you as a person? Am I no better than I was twenty or thirty years ago? I held my tongue and pondered what he'd said and what he'd really meant.

I believe that life moves around us enriching us, depleting us, providing wisdom, taking hope. We battle, we win, and sometimes we don't. I believe Aciman would agree that at my core, I am still the woman who scared the raccoon down the alley to protect my family. I am still the woman who told my father-in-law he could no longer live with us. And I am still the woman who told Jean-Luc to go back to Paris, that he could no longer stay in our home. At my core, the instinct to protect my family will always outweigh my natural compassion for others—especially anyone who threatens the safety of my precious ones—regardless of the consequences.

What were my consequences? I have carried the weight of regret, confusion, and uncertainty for years. When I first read them, Sébastien's words stabbed me as I had imagined Jean-Luc's dagger might. I staggered, but then I embraced them. I took the words to heart—much like a martyr.

I should have done better.

I thought I was the protector. However, in the story Jean-Luc told, that modern-day Bluebeard placed the blame squarely on me. And I accepted it.

But the passage of time is often accompanied by wisdom: I was the protector—of my own. I no longer accept the blame for Jean-Luc's unhappy American adventure. He came damaged, and he left damaged. Fuck Sébastien.

A month after Jean-Luc returned to Paris, my son received a message from him via Facebook. He advised my son to never trust women. Especially his mother.

Sweet.

Now, let me set the record straight, and my son is fully aware: Mothers protect. Be they mama rats or humans. It's what they do. Especially this mother.

Heat Map

Hannah Hindley

HOW TO BEGIN WHEN THE BEGINNING MATTERS THE LEAST? DID IT HAPPEN ON a boat with an ex-boyfriend who had forgotten, in the time that had passed between us, what my body liked? Did it happen in a Seattle hotel room? I had spent the night there with a man from my captain's class who I wasn't particularly attracted to but who seemed gentle, and so I stayed, and so I took him between my legs, and so I drank orange juice with him among the businessmen in the shining lobby the next morning.

I remember how tired I felt when I arrived in Missoula that fall in search of a graduate program—how I ordered chai and nursed the caffeine out of it in the low light of the late afternoons. It snowed while I was there, though it did not stick, and I bundled up and felt slow and lonely.

I remember the long drive back to my childhood home in California, drinking gas station iced tea and yerba mate out of cans in order to stay alert at the wheel, dragging hours of *The Goldfinch* on audiobook. Craggy passes gave way to pine forests gave way to oak woodland.

I remember sharp cramping—how finely tuned my attention to it was, while the rest of my body perched quietly in the driver's seat.

I remember waiting for my period. I remember waiting, beginning to worry. Counting backward through the weeks in my mind.

I remember buying the test next to the condoms at CVS, how I threw in some almonds and shampoo with the purchase to make it feel somehow routine and casual. A navigable thing.

I read the instructions three times to make sure I did it properly. I remember the blue lines, perpendicular, a faint but unmistakable "plus."

I DIDN'T WANT A baby. I went about the business of taking care of it with the same remove that I approached medical emergencies in my wilderness guiding job. Stop the blood. Check for unseen damage. Package and evacuate. Once the gears of disaster are set in motion, it's easy to remain calm.

I knew that there were pills available to induce an abortion, but my work schedule threw off the odds of it succeeding. Medical abortions require a follow-up appointment to ensure the chemicals have done their work. I'd be leaving in a handful of days to fly to Hawaii for a two-month boat job. With an hour or so ashore every week, it seemed like a stretch to seek out an appointment in Kona. And what if the pills didn't take?

Instead, I called and made an appointment for a clinical abortion with my hometown gynecologist. The process—a consultation followed by a later insertion of a dilating sponge into the cervix followed by a surgical abortion the day after that—would be over in time for my travels. This isn't how every abortion proceeds. Although insurance did not cover my procedure, I didn't have to fight for mine, didn't have to cross state lines, didn't have to wade through protestors in front of a public clinic, and I knew how lucky this made me. It was 2016. My rights still felt infallible.

I am, by nature, private. I choose to go about my choices quietly and independently. But I was staying in my mother's house that Thanksgiving, where she could see my comings and goings. Reluctantly, I told her what was happening.

"You should cancel your work contract," she said. "It takes time to bounce back from an abortion."

But I imagine I probably rolled my eyes. I have always been even-keeled and buoyant. I wasn't about to let an unwanted pregnancy derail me.

IN 1671, JANE SHARP published *The Midwives Book*. She instructed women how to maintain their pregnancies from conception to childbirth and after. She also used the book as a platform to express her views on women's education, male physicians, and female sexuality. In Jane's first edition, she included plants that would cause a miscarriage. By the time the fourth edition was published in 1725, any mention of "miscarriage" herbs was omitted, but what remained was a list of plants that could be used to induce menses: "artemisia, tansy, pennyroyal and catnip, taken with cinnamon water." Perhaps editors removed contentious abortive remedies from the volume after Jane's death, but the purpose of these herbs still glimmers in the subtext: an induced period, without question, will flush the uterus clean.

BEFORE MY MOTHER DROVE me to my gynecologist's office, I swallowed two pills—an opioid and an antibiotic—and dressed myself in front of the bedroom mirror.

At the office, the nurse practitioner asked me if I was still certain about the decision, and I told her I was. Was I supposed to have doubts?

In the operation room, I stripped down again and donned a crinkly medical gown, open at the back. As I waited, I shivered a little and looked around the polished room. Spiraled cords slung down from wall-mounted equipment that looked like it had lived there since the seventies. A speculum sat on a gleaming tray next to a tube of lubricant; tall jars held swab sticks, tongue depressors, cotton balls.

I lay with my heels in stirrups, with my legs turned open under the gown. My gynecologist talked me through the process, but I still tensed at the entry of the speculum, at its coldness, at the horrific cranking widening that it brought. I still tensed at the tug of the tools as the dilating sponge (made from seaweed) was removed from my cervix. I tensed at the painful entry of the suction tube, the muffled movements inside of myself that slurped the uterus clean. My gynecologist counted aloud the seconds that remained, and then the wand slid back out, the speculum cranked shut, my toes uncurled.

I was left alone to dress. I used a paper towel to wipe away excess lubricant, and as I pulled my underwear back on, I noticed a large glass vessel on the floor next to the operating table, filled with dark fluid, spattered with my blood.

PENNYROYAL GREW WILD ALONG the coastal trails that I walked as a child. Its neatly stacked purple blooms swayed like pompoms in the fog; when crushed in hand, they smelled like eucalyptus oil and mint. It's related to peppermint, but it's poison if you eat it, my mom would tell me.

When I took my first job in a national park, I would hike in the foothills outside of Yosemite and collect mugwort—*Artemisia douglasiana*—where it grew near the poppies and the dripping banks of live-forevers. I'd dry it and steep it into dream-inducing tea, hoping for visions but mostly just enjoying the hot mug of wild leaves between my palms. At night, with the Artemisia laid out to dry, my room filled with the smell of wet dirt and spice.

WHEN I ARRIVED IN Hawaii, I was still bleeding, but I leaned into the work at hand. I hauled heavy anchor chain onto the windlass, launched kayaks off the back deck of the boat, and told stories to passengers about fish and sea birds. I moved greasily through the engine room, tossed by big waves, nauseous in the generator's roar. Although I buckled over with seasickness, although my stomach emptied as ten-foot seas rocked me from one hot wall to another below deck, I was grateful that the nausea was traceable.

Untraceable, though, was an imprecise sadness that would catch up to me on certain evenings. I would stay up late on bridge watch, watching the lights from night dive boats way out where the lip of the

Big Island dropped off into the miles-deep Pacific. In the other direction, the volcanic contour of the land rose up black against the blackness of the sky. 'Ōhi'a lehua seedlings unfurled, unseen in the night, out of that raw and ropelike lava rock.

I'd sit next to the mate, both of us looking outward. I'd think about lost loves, think about loneliness, cycle through heavy failures that I'd forgotten were my own. A tight despair pressed against my skull, my chest, the door of my windpipe. I hoped, in the faint flash of light from the dive boats, that the mate couldn't see the wetness on my face from where he sat in the darkened bridge.

A COUPLE YEARS BACK, a committee of diverse experts assembled by the National Academies of Sciences, Engineering, and Medicine published a report that says the four major abortion methods used in the US—medication, aspiration, induction, and dilation and evacuation—are all safe and effective, and that complications are rare. It was the first report of its kind since 1975, and the most rigorous review the country has yet seen. The groundbreaking 186-page review also concluded that evidence generally does not suggest that abortions increase a woman's risk of mental health conditions such as depression, anxiety, and post-traumatic stress disorder.

THAT SUMMER, MY JOB carried me away from Hawaii and into Alaska. As a guide, this was normal—exchanging one landscape for another, carrying my possessions in a backpack, following work wherever the change of seasons pushed it. The peaks and low places that I moved through for work, I began to apprehend, were far more hospitable than the alien new topographies rolling under my skin.

I remember sitting by the Kennecott River one night while a bonfire lit up the shore across the way. Up-valley, a glacial plug had burst and a summer's worth of meltwater was draining out in one catastrophic torrent. Ambulance-sized blocks of ice slammed and shuddered against the bridge downstream from me. I sat with my loneliness under the dark glacier, let my desolation expand. I considered walking into the river. I wondered how long I'd be able to stand in the battering gray water before it knocked me into its current. I wondered how far my body might be carried before they found it.

I remember walking uphill on another night, climbing home to where I lived that summer in a wall tent on a ridge. The sun had just set, and though I could not see National Creek where it cut down through a gorge above town, I could hear it tumbling darkly next to me. My footsteps were heavy, and a rising despair pressurized my ribcage, tightened the back of my throat. I sobbed and sobbed. I would walk a small distance and then drag to a stop, walk again then stop, sitting among muddy roots that coiled and crisscrossed like hospital cables. The climb ahead felt impossible.

At the top of the hill, where wind and mosquitos and starlight moved through the gaps in my tent, my bed waited for me. Where the edges of the tent grazed the ground grew tangled summer flowers: fireweed, bluebells, fragrant silver-green sprays of wild Artemisia.

YOU DON'T JUST BOUNCE back from an abortion, my mother had said.

She met my dad in 1973. A couple of months into their relationship, she discovered that she was pregnant; together, they agreed that it was too soon to raise a child. My mom made an appointment at an abortion clinic in Boston. It was likely freshly painted, likely freshly strung with coiled cords and humming with new pneumatics. It was the year of *Roe v. Wade*.

When she walked back out, the problem was gone, but for months afterward, my mother lived in a sort of emotional fog.

"It was no time to have a child, but I was really surprised how it affected me," she tells me when I ask about it over the phone. She was listless for a long time after the decision. I push her to explain the source of her depression. She says she thinks about it still: How old would that child be now? Would it be a boy or a girl? She imagines the sadness that she felt might have been a kind of spiritual pain. From the moment of conception, there's a bond that begins to form between mother and child. It hurts to break that bond, she reflects.

"But at the time, is that what it *felt* like?" I ask. "Spiritual pain?"

She pauses on the other end of the line. "All I can say is, something was gone that was highly creative and joyful."

Online (read: non-scientific) sources will confirm my mother's emotional story: women who abort or miscarry can experience staggering sadness, despite official reports that suggest otherwise. In my searches, the explanation surfaces time and again: the depression comes from shock, grief, the breaking of a bond. Of *course*, the support sites insist, it is natural to feel morose.

But these explanations hit flat for me. I feel confident that, unlike my mother, grief is not quite the thing I felt.

I've never dreamed of having a child. As a wilderness guide, I make pennies. I've rarely lived in the same place longer than a year. I don't covet other women's newborns or lie awake devising baby names. I break up with men who do not vote, unerringly, for women's rights.

When I first visited my gynecologist's office, he performed an ultrasound on me. "Do you want to see it?" he asked. I wasn't particularly interested, but I looked up, for the sake of science. There it was onscreen, a little yolk, a black roundness in my womb that had expanded secretively inside of me for six weeks.

I wanted it out.

I do not think about the procedure itself—my decision, the removal of that yolk—as a spiritual dilemma. A thousand alternate universes in which I had to make the choice, and I would make the same choice again, every time.

But following my abortion, nowhere could I find explanations or research that helped pinpoint the source of the hopelessness I was feeling. Placations about motherly grief felt misplaced and imprecise.

At sea and in the mountains, in deep rainforest and along the open blue tongues of glaciers, I knew to consult maps that could show me where I'd come from and what lay ahead. The route I was walking after my abortion had been traveled by numberless women before me. Still, no one, it seemed, had yet drawn up a navigable chart.

WHEN I TEACH COLLEGE writing classes, I show maps to my students. In one of them, glowing routes zigzag and loop across dark cities, dark continents. The Strava heatmap shows where people walk (or bike, or swim). Each person's track shows up as a sparkling arc. And out of the black land, well-traveled paths begin to emerge. People retrace their steps, follow the same routes that others have already walked. Certain tracks on the heatmap become bold, chiseled (a running trail, a central bike lane). They glow like fire. As if looking down on illuminated cities from an airplane, the viewer begins to perceive patterns in that neon tangle of movement.

My heat travels interior paths, too. Hormones ferry through my bloodstream, carrying messages from one cell to another. *Be scared,* they say. *Be happy.* Blood sluices out of my heart into the corners of the body and muscles back home again through tapestries of veins. The blood vessels in my body, extracted and strung out valve to valve, would stretch a hundred thousand miles long.

Last year, my blood thickened along the walls of my uterus, darkly filled a glass container next to a surgical bed. Blood travels extraordinary routes. If illuminated as a heat map, it, too, might appear tangled. It, too, might reveal uncanny patterns.

On the boats where my guiding work carries me, mapping is more than an academic curiosity. At sea, triangulation is the process by which wayfarers find their position using visible landmarks. A navigator will take compass bearings on landmarks and then trace those bearings backward along a map. Looking out at an unfamiliar dark sea, a sailor looks for recognizable things that match her chart. She might inscribe the angle toward a known lighthouse, toward a navigation buoy, toward the outer edge of an island. The navigator can be certain that she is somewhere within that tightly drawn triangle, in the space where those lines intersect on the page.

How to triangulate when the brain is the foreign country, the body the dark sea? What landmarks can be trusted in the country of blood and bone?

I go looking for those landmarks, looking for bridges between unwieldy emotions and the mappable mechanisms of the brain. I dig for charts and diagrams, for visual answers to unseen things. In graph after graph, I watch how hormone production in the uterus does nothing but rise as a pregnancy advances. When the fetus aborts, when the graph line falls, there is no hormonal parachute to slow the crash. What effect does this have on brains, on bodies? I can't find that research; perhaps it doesn't exist. Historically—and especially with stigmatized events like abortions and miscarriages—women seldom take center stage in health studies. But scientists have looked at plummeting hormones during menopause. In those studies, they've found that estrogen affects mood across the whole brain's topography.

The amygdala—responsible for primal emotions, for mood—has one of the highest densities of estrogen anywhere in the brain. Rats show a dramatic drop in depressive symptoms when estrogen is injected into the amygdala. In fact, the whole limbic system—the part of the brain where our emotions and memories live—thrives in the presence of estrogen: neurogenesis ramps up, mood elevates, emotions calm. A recent psychiatric study on menopause shows that estrogen balances and safeguards our nerves, our brains.

The other major sex hormone, progesterone, also has a calming effect. When levels drop low, serotonin production decreases, too. Women with low levels of progesterone can experience depression and anxiety.

And here's the thing: for six weeks, my body began building a sticky placental wall for a fetus to fold into, began ramping up both progesterone and estrogen production. My amygdala, my hypothalamus, my hippocampus all sizzled alive. Lab rats were given a similar eight-week treatment of estrogen and progesterone. When the treatment ended, the rats' hypothalami spat with disturbance; the animals slinked into depressive behavior.

I am not a scientist, although I admire them. I can only pull together the things I find and arrange them, one by one, next to the things I have felt. I feel, sometimes, like a blind cartographer. But I look to new mothers, too, and I can trace this same hormonal rise and crash in their experiences, also.

Decades of research have failed to neatly identify the root causes of postpartum depression, but we have begun to learn—through animal studies—that sex hormones are linked tightly to the condition. Rats flooded with estrogen and progesterone and then shoved into a state of hormonal withdrawal akin to childbirth will lapse, like the rats in the menopause study, into depression. They stop swimming when forced into tanks of water: a behavioral indicator of despair. They ramp up their sugar consumption—a behavioral indicator of anhedonia: the inability to feel pleasure.

Up to 20 percent of women who have carried a pregnancy through to birth will experience postpartum depression in the hours, or days, or months after having a child. Their symptoms: a persistent depressed mood for long stretches of time, a loss of interest in activities previously considered pleasurable, hopelessness, despair, lethargy, feelings of worthlessness, thoughts of suicide.

Whether blobby yolk or living child, when our bellies break clean of the thing they've carried, our hearts—which is to say, our hormones—can misfire, stumble, rage against our selves.

And still, in research where more often than not men are the ones who hold the tools, answers still evade us. To be clear, science pushes unequivocally toward truth. But it can push, also, against stories of individuals in favor of tidier averages.

Meanwhile, in the flush of hormones, in the circuitry of blood, my body becomes its own unruly atlas.

As I TRAVELED THOSE new topographies in the year following my abortion, friends joined me for certain distances. They walked with me, sometimes, along the trails that I followed into myself.

Leslie drove me to the natural foods store. "I don't know what's happening and I can't pull myself out," I'd told her. "There are so many days when I'd be OK with dying."

It had been months already since the procedure. Leslie understood sadnesses that would not lift. She curled up tightly every winter when the days got short. Shelf by shelf, we rifled through the familiar bottles that she kept in her own toolkit. 5-HTP. St. John's Wort. Skullcap. Eleuthero. Rescue Remedy. Ashwagandha. I gathered them all into my basket. In the months to come, I swallowed pills and tinctures, teas and tablets that dissolved like snow under my tongue.

Amary called often to check in on me. She understood that depression, like grief, doesn't go let itself out of the house when it sees that it has overstayed its welcome. She knew that these things took time. "You're usually so good at being happy," she said. "Is it any better? Has it lifted? Stop being a fucking animal and reach out when it's bad," she said. "I'm *here*."

"The hormonal changes of pregnancy and the postpartum period do not occur in isolation," one study says. What it means to say is, we contain interconnected circuitries, organs, impulses. The ravages of hormone fluctuation don't go about their business independently from the messy rest of the body. Body, as in oneself. Body, as in a large area of water or land or ice on a map. Body, as in a substantial amount of a thing: a body of folklore, a body of evidence. Body, as in a group of people with a common purpose. How far outward do those interconnected circuitries bleed? The heatmap sparks with overlapping footfall. Changes do not occur in isolation.

I think of the women all down the long back alley of history, the ones who leaned into one another, forehead to forehead. I think of the midwives who were brave about naming herbs in their books. I think of the midwives who, later, were burned, and hung, and drowned for harvesting the pennyroyal from where it grew in the damp ditches outside of town. I think of the women whose tintype pictures show up in the archives of asylums: committed for hysterics, from the Greek *hustera*: womb, uterus. I think of my friend Merilee, as seen in a cell phone picture taken in a foreign port where she, with other female crewmembers, waits behind bars—their ship is a traveling abortion clinic, carrying misoprostol, the abortion pill, to countries where it is not legal. I think of the women who didn't have one another, who bled dead from trying to scrape out the unwanted yolk all on their own.

I think of my mother.

If, as she believes, a spiritual pain is felt after an abortion from some breaking of a bond, I consider the female bonds that might help heal that rift.

MOSTLY, THOUGH, I CONSIDER chemicals and synapses and secretions: the heavy facts of sadness divorced from any narrative of grief. I think about the gappy medical reports where heart and hormone are left unconsidered.

Who gets to ask the questions? What hasn't yet been asked?

In political circles that advocate for abortion bans, a psychological condition is often mentioned: post-abortion stress disorder, or PASS. It shares many of the same mental symptoms as post-traumatic stress disorder: anxiety, numbness, depression, and suicidal thoughts. The kinship makes sense: trauma comes in all sizes, after all. But there is no mention of PASS in the recent 186-page report on the safety of abortion, and the condition cannot be found in the annals of the American Psychiatric Association or the American Psychological Association. Some psychologists argue that the term was invented as a political tool: pseudo-science to further leverage the agenda against a woman's right to choose what's best for her own body. But the symptoms of PASS don't feel bogus or contrived. They match closely with my own. What does it mean when the ugly powers that have worked so hard to invalidate my bodily autonomy are the only ones who are willing to name my bodily experience in clean and recognizable medical terms?

PASS is dismissed by psychologists as a non-condition, but it shouldn't be. Abortions are vital, and they're also complicated and messy and hard. No one should have to enter such well-traveled territory without a roadmap. The right to safe recovery is as essential as the right to safe abortion.

In the *Roe v. Wade* battleground that lies ahead in this nation, we should be having these conversations: how to defend our hearts as well as our rights. How to prioritize deep attention to the female experience in scientific and medical studies. How to secure both infallible autonomy *and* infallible care for all bodies, from the uterus to the limbic system and the complicated self that unites them. Until our science catches up with the full experience of the female body, it makes sense that our politics will fail us, too.

I LOOK BACK THROUGH Jane Sharp's garden of abortifacients. She tells us to mix our herbs with cinnamon water. We now know that cinnamon—rufous and fragrant—inhibits various proteins associated with stress responses, depression, and a sense of hopelessness. On Jane's list, too: pennyroyal—liquid extracts of which are useful for depression—and catnip, which eases anxiety, elevates mood, and promotes sleep.

Artemisia—mugwort—is named after Artemis, the Greek moon goddess and patron of women. It is, they say, the bitterest of all the herbs. But as tea and as tincture, it nourishes the nervous system, calms depression, and protects against nightmares. This, too, is listed in Jane's abortion garden.

Bound up in the crushed handfuls of herbs that wash yolk from womb are the implicit remedies for the nightmare that can follow. Jane Sharp had quietly built a map, sprinkled seeds along the route, sewn the topographic contours with purple blooms and bitter roots.

ONE EVENING LAST SUMMER, I stepped outside of my tent and moved among the bobbing buds of highbush cranberry, saxifrage, mugwort. The glacier in the valley below me had scraped the land raw, and a slow crust of new life—dryas, alder, lichen—shimmered at the edges of the devastation.

I pinched off some mugwort and crushed its silver leaves with sour cranberries, stirred them into my gin. I waited to see what might regrow in the sparse country of my self.

heart circle

M. Kate Allen

no
is a complete sentence
the crone says
without apology

I gape
exasperated
    guilt
   curiosity
  wonder
rippling across my flesh
like geese
winging their way forward

the crone would have us believe that
every no is a decisive waymarker
for the migration

I say nothing
I will judge for myself

meanwhile
the crone cracks a sage smile
meeting me eye to eye
I feel naked suddenly

not merely that

I feel shame at being seen
and I look away

we look around
nerves crackling
fiery divinities forming an unlikely circle
willingly holding ample space
for each woman's weird ways
discovering we are all dreamers here
wending our way in
to the ever-fertile womb of the unknown
a damp place where shadows dance in the velvet dark of desire
and seeds ache to grow

together
  with
    mouths
      closed

with
  eyes
    ears
      arms
        open

we bear witness to the Goddess who weaves the story of her becoming

    she is
      her own
        well of wisdom
      her own
         source of light
      her own
        cauldron of alchemy

    we witness
    her glory emerging
    each of us perceiving
    that the honor of wholehearted attention we give
    is the honor we will receive in turn

    looking upon myself at last

I am

    breath taken with ecstasy

    I catch the crone eyeing me again
    and this time I hold her gaze
    which sparkles madly with delight

    late that night
    as I await Aurora's brushstrokes in the Sonoran sky
    the stars mirror the brilliant singularity
    I call I

of course
no
is a complete sentence

the one seeking explanation of this word made flesh
will receive no further answer from me

perhaps in this silence
the seeker will hear the beat
of her own wild heart

and meet the reflection of starlight
in my eyes

Brass

Ingrid L. Taylor

Baba Yaga's Brothel

Are you surprised to see me here?
This hoary crone, a traceless scandal
whose birch barked trail has traversed a dozen worlds,
you shudder at my crevassed grin.
Is the promise of fig-ripe flesh enough
to gird your courage?
My girls are healthy as the morning dew, starched
& buttoned, with pristine skirts to cover
their clawed feet.

Never mind how the prairie groans and wails around you.
Never mind how we writhe beneath you. Your blood and cum
stain the open grasses, & your rank scent turns
the coyote from his path. You wanted it wild—
let me give you something to tame.

Do not mistake my acumen for generosity
or your greed for destiny. We will set spurs to your groin
& kindle our flames inside your skull. We've measured
the depths of bruises, how they tunnel to
pierce the heart. How they crosshatch and scar
the landscapes of flesh and loam.

You see, I know about blades & iron teeth,
the way they dig deep to sever spines
& make pieced meals of a whole.

Return your coin to your pocket—your brass
means nothing to me.

I demand of you this:

Walk barefoot into the wilderness
see the hare pause midflight
in tremulous attention, listen
to the grasslands chant
an ageless incantation
composed before you ever dreamed
of wheat and gold.

Stand until the moon climbs and swells with the wolf's
howl & the mice emerge from their woven nests,
until the sun rises again, & the sounds of crickets enter
your mouth and swarm your entire body,
& you are only joyous chirp and rustling meadow
and fur and tooth and talon under a high bright sky.

Come back to me
& tell me

what it is
you think you own.

Middle Bear

Vanessa Rowan Whitfield

It all begins with the wildness of being born a girl;
cubbish we had all conspired to take over the world.
Oversized hats and shoes too big and throats tied with Mother's pearls.
Hairy and scary we growl in mirrors with little legs and kneecaps like burls.

Climbing down from moonlit tree top and running through agrestal floors,
wearing bushy hides (like capes on napes) of the ones who came before.
Yellow apples grow heavy on sky stuck branches and fall into purses we wore,
Ursine queens, we collect all the pelts, and will never grow old, so we roared.

It happens suddenly to us while we are done up in our consuming costume.
All in a moment the change begins while we are at our most groomed.
Capable bodies both able and sable, manicured and dripping in perfume.
Dwindling pheromones replaced by spices, doused in the aura of heavy fumes.

We are at our tallest on hind leg, our bodies become full with fur,
Our memory begins to falter until we forget everything we ever were.
Signing papers at gilded buildings and leaving keys with chauffeur,
The way we once used our senses to dig up roots to heal becomes a blur.

Hibernating in silken sleep mask, I roll over in my Tempur pedic bed.

Ovulating is a fleeting thing left unsaid, I wake up with a hangover instead.

Celebrating another morning with gourmet sandwiches and soaking my
middle spread.

Congregating with bubbles and oils and a pile of books I have not yet read.

Too tired to climb anymore trees and getting too warm to the touch to nuzzle,

I coat my snout in pretty powders and do face yoga on my drooping muzzle.

An evening well spent with aromatic scents, and a vintage crossword puzzle.

On less bread do I dine with low carb I align, all these supplements and elixirs
I guzzle.

Belly full and fermented, stuffed with berries and fruits fed from polished claw.

My mouth is covered in sweet honeycomb, licking the residue from my paws.

My innards crammed with saccharin jams, ambrosia funneled through
made up maw.

Venus Ursa of my bathtub, rose water steam and petals forgo any flaws.

Wrapping arms around myself in quiet, I embrace the embrace of bruin,

I scan the dents and dimples of my body, relics of reconstruction and old ruin.

The sound of something rustling can be heard as I brush this body that I
grew in.

Little cave woman wearing the cloak of her Mama waits for me to shed my
own skin.

The Club

Liz Kelner Pozen

Bad guys are still here.
They can be anywhere
but seem to have been relegated
to less public areas—
better for hiding?
Or perhaps they have finally
learned their place.

The club fights villains.
Now working on a special case,
each member
has her own suitcase
full of useful supplies—
a soft blanket
an extra headband
a smooth rock
with calming properties.

My job as the newest member
is to distract evil doers—
maybe by sticking out a foot
to trip them.

Since I am not sure how to
recognize the enemies,
she creates a special signal—
two hands together
fluttering like a butterfly—
to announce their approach.

It is serious
secret business
which I respect
in my pleasure
at having passed some
unknown test
admitting me
to this select group
of seven year olds
trying to sort out the world.

Putting Down a Horse

Marie A. Unini

TODAY I WILL PUT DOWN MY MARE, BAHIANA. "PUT DOWN," ALWAYS SUCH AN ambiguous term for me, every time I hear it used. I think, no, there is something better, something more exact. "Put down" is what you do with your knife and fork at the end of a meal. You put down the baby for a nap. Put down a rebellion. Put down someone by way of insult. But putting down as a way of ending life, well, I know what the dictionary says, but it just doesn't ever resonate with me. But "euthanize." Now there's a prettier euphemism. But it's all the same. I must order her compassionate death by injection.

There are choices, naturally. "Let nature take its course," that's a good one. You can't just allow a dog with cancer, or a cat with kidney failure, or a horse who can't stand, to just languish and fade in nature's own good time. Who could do that? Were this a human proposition, we would call in hospice, get support from social workers and nurses, hire caregivers. That's what I did for my mother, when it was clear that she did not want to move forward in this life. Told the doctors, "No more treatment." Isn't that somehow equivalent to "put her down"? I don't know where the greater mercy lies. But I must make some phone calls.

"You're going to want to get things ready, Marie," Steve said as he was packing up his horse-shoeing tools two weeks ago. "Here," he said, guiding my hand, "feel her legs." They are hot, not the normal cool they should be. "One day soon, you're going to come out here and find her down, she won't want to get up. It'll be too painful for her to stand.

You don't want to be taken by surprise."

He's telling me what I know and don't want to face, that my twenty-nine-year-old mare is at the end of her life, that her chronic ligament inflammation from an old injury is no longer treatable, and I need to make the preparations to end it for her. Put her down. It is not a simple, single-act—it's a project requiring several coordinated working parts, anticipation, and planning. I need to get started right away; I know. And I don't. You could call this denial. So yes, I will be taken by surprise.

My work life has been busy, and yes, I've been meaning to make those phone calls, get everything lined up, but of course today—the day that I decided I would finally have time to do it all—today is the day I walk from the house to the corral, and find her lying down, a Sphinx, half upright, forelegs curved under, her devoted sidekick Calypso hovering, vigilant. I'm not too late, of course, but this event signals urgency that eclipses all other demands of the day.

Three phone calls: the vet, the brothers with the backhoe, and my closest friend. Connie is the hardest. She will want to come immediately, hover over me that way Calypso does Bahiana, waiting for me to show need, to do the thing that rarely happens that aggrieves her so in its absence. Support me. She thinks I closed my heart years ago, when my brother died. "You've changed, Unini. You are not the friend I knew." She's half right, perhaps. What shows on the outside changed, and maybe that affected what's felt on the inside, a bit. But I do still feel, really I do. I just can't let it interfere with what must be done. That's what I did when Eddie died. I got busy taking care of what needed doing, and taking care of the people who didn't seem like they were going to make it through this tragedy intact. My parents. The man who felt responsible for the accident. The woman who didn't want to blame him. I grounded them, a lightning rod for their emotions. And I guess I just kept being busy, like an engine that hasn't been turned off, always on idle. That's what she sees. She remembers the "before" me—the wilder, uncensored one, and she keeps lamenting its absence. And when she does, she's the last person I want support from, because that noisy longing for me to be some way other than I am is attached to it. And it drains me, distracts me from the doing.

We are wired differently. Tears erupt for her at the smallest provocation—talking about her estranged siblings is a good one, children in cages at the border a certain one. I was not crying, by force of habit, long before my brother died. She requires support, often dramatically, demands it even. Once, she called at 6 in the morning and told me she couldn't get out of bed, and would I please come. She lived on an isolated alfalfa ranch in the high desert north of Los Angeles. She didn't do well with the isolation sometimes. I drove eighty miles, made Mexican hot chocolate for us both, and climbed into bed with her. We speculated about what could possibly get her up and moving again, and shortly a brightly colored hot air balloon—tourists who had drifted off course—landed in the field closest to us. She declared it a miracle, and got out of bed, fully restored.

But right now, what I really want to do, I just want to sit down with Bahiana. I don't want to awaken Bob. Nothing. No calls, not yet. It's 6:30 a.m., quiet as only our dirt road cul-de-sac can be, a light breeze brushing over us from the east. The earth is still cool to the touch from the night. I give Calypso his morning feed, and he wanders off, but continues to glance at us between mouthfuls. I sit down and lean against her—something that would have been impossible before. She sighs and stares at me. Take your time, she seems to say. Twenty-nine years of memory wash through me: how tiny she seemed at six months, just barely my height, how trusting she was, and patient, how ignorant I was—a first-timer who had no business with a horse. Our great adventures, how she took care of me, rather than the reverse. The time I got us into a tight passage, believing we were going to emerge into a larger box canyon, how she backed us out and side-stepped up an almost vertical slope, gently letting me slip out of the saddle, and scrambled back down while I slid behind her. The first time I knew that she read my thoughts, riding bareback and I thought about turning right, and she did. Feeling that connection pass between our skins.

Bahiana was fifteen when we brought Calypso to live with us, and they merged in a classic mare/gelding bond: she led, he followed and doted, attached to her like a perpetual son to mother. Some of this is herd habit, but with them it was more their personal chemistry. She was bossy. He was mellow. When we rode, if you didn't keep him fully collected, he would relax his neck so low that his lips would drag on the ground. Being groomed, he would doze off, standing. He was trusting and liked people. But his connection to Bahiana was fierce. If I took her out without him, he would pace as we left and whinny until we were out of earshot. He would often stand there, as if rooted, until we came back in range again—which could sometimes be an hour or more—and then, when he sensed our proximity, which could be a quarter mile, he'd start up again, mumbling and clearing his throat.

I have known her longer than I knew my brother, longer than most of my friends. I don't want to call anyone, I wish we could just do this alone, Bahiana and I. I wish I could just lie here with her and feel her slip away. We sit for an hour or more like this, and when Bob comes out to feed and discovers us, I have nearly drifted off in daydream. I make the calls.

Dr. Marteney tells me to let him know when I've got the backhoe on site, and wherever he is, he promises, he won't be more than thirty minutes away. The Clutter brothers arrive and begin digging where I indicate, one of them managing the enormous tractor and scoop with the delicacy of a surgeon and his tools, the other measuring and directing. Connie arrives, asks what I need, I say I don't know, just be here. I'm glad that you are. She examines me. I have cried, a little, but not so much that you would know. She positions herself at a short distance outside the corral and shifts her weight from one foot to the other, her nervous little dance.

Bob asks what we should do with Calypso, who is now on high alert. "Do you want him to see this?" I hesitate. Without waiting for my response, he halters him and takes him to the far west side of the corral, behind a dense screen of juniper trees, perhaps fifty feet away and out of sight of what Marteney and I will do, and the backhoe after us.

Marteney asks me if I'm ready. He is usually so chatty, big energy presence. Making small talk about politics; complaining about the young vets just out of school, and how they don't know how to work, don't want to; imagining all the golfing he will do when he retires, someday, if he could just find a replacement for the seven-day-a-week, twenty-four-hour emergency on-call business that he has spoiled us all with. Always someday. Today he is soft, slow, calm. I feel his sadness. No, I joke, could we just press rewind and start our relationship all over? He smiles. "You're going to have to get her to stand, Marie. We can't do this when they're lying down, too much danger of them thrashing." As if on cue, Bahiana stirs and stiffly presses herself up onto all four legs. It leaves her a little breathless, and so we wait. He administers the first injection, a kind of horse valium that he uses to relax them when he files their teeth. She sighs and begins to sway ever so gently. The second injection is effective, and in such a surprising, graceful way, this thousand-pound animal sinks in soft folds to the ground, like a dropped heavy linen dinner napkin. This all feels so peaceful to me, and now I'm crying, tears of relief, and Marteney places an arm across my shoulders. And then I hear it, from the west, beyond the screen of junipers. A wail, a howl, a high full-throated bellow, an other-worldly trembling of enormous vocal cords, and it drives right down into me, lightning seeking ground. Bob will later tell me that he knew exactly what we were doing, and when, because Calypso began to pace and circle, pawing, pulling toward where we were, and he knew, when he cried out, that it was done.

The Clutters complete their impossibly gentle, delicate job, and Connie joins me to stand by Bahiana's fresh grave. She has brought a bright bouquet of plastic flowers from Vallarta Market, in a small plastic vase that she sets in the middle of the large circle of fresh dirt, whose brightness will miraculously survive the elements for two years. She opens her arms to me, and she is crying, of course. My precious loving surrogate. And I step into them, and I feel my own grounding in there, in that embrace.

The Body of a Bird

Elise Ball

The day we buried it, we forgot to bring the wine
so we loved ourselves through feeling affected
by the mundane and allowing it; the drums
in our chests growing bigger or smaller, further away
or very close up, thumping
on a loop. The dirt is not the bottom,
but the beginning. One small bug
eats another; layers of living
off each other, swelling
plump and full. You have to look
with profound respect
to see it.

I'd been searching for an owl unsuccessfully
and all the season there were cardinals,
chickadees and sparrows
in the mimosa. Among their covered bones
is the same silk scripture
inside an eggshell. Birds know it
upon birthing. Then they fly off, and unlike us
do not forget.

Aching for More

Armen Bacon

Bad things happened.

My plane was hijacked.

A best friend ghosted me.

I fell, crushing my shoulder.

Slept with my boss.

Lost the luggage.

Missed connecting flights.

Woke up in a foreign gutter.

Scorched my corneas.

Buried my son.

Lost my faith.

Left France for the States.

Not necessarily in that order.

Growing restless and fidgety during my junior year of college, I relocated to France (a broad studying abroad) for one entire year. I ate baguettes smothered with Brie and ripened Camembert. My morning ritual included warm croissants and pain chocolate fresh out of a patisserie oven. I gained 22 kilos and grew two cup sizes, sipping café au lait by day, drinking wine by dusk—until thoughts slurred with uncanny fluency. Mastering idioms and slang expressions like *Merde alors, Je m'en fou,* and *Ce que je m'en fiche,* even foreigners thought of me as a local.

My inner gypsy, a not-so-quiet, persistent voice nagging from within, handed me the world. Hungry to dance and twirl, she pushed me into the arms of handsome men, conniving gigolos, even a few offspring of the rich and famous—one in particular, whose father, he swore, was a world famous symphony conductor. He played me like a well-rehearsed concerto, fingering my senses first lightly in minor notes then with staccato precision. The entire concert lasted only minutes but was accentuated by a full moon, a hot summer night in Monaco, and two beating hearts.

Little by little, the gypsy's secret fantasies became mine—transporting me to Morocco, Greece, Italy, and Spain; Turkey, South Africa, Portugal, and Tunisia. The map now hanging in my office resembles a throbbing pincushion on the verge of erupting. Hiding beneath it—an inconspicuous file folder of notes and names, each encased with hearts drawn in purple ink: Jean Louis, Pierre, Miguel, Antoine, Nikko, Renaldo.

Who was this woman who loved to brag about peeing in the Danube, making love behind the Trevi Fountain, hitchhiking her way through Europe, North Africa, and the Middle East? With every detail perfectly scripted, she recounts the time she was mugged and robbed on a night train headed to Florence. *Women should never take night trains solo,* her chaperones had warned. But at twenty-one, she knew it all and possessed a flair for defiance.

Three years later, while soaring at 35,000 feet, her plane was hijacked by a madman escaping from a mental institution in Atascadero. Without announcing his plan to passengers, the pilot performed a mid-air stall to catch the man off balance while many screamed at the top of their lungs or recited the Rosary. As the jetliner plummeted thousands of feet, fearing the end was near, she grabbed a pair of hands neatly folded in the lap next to hers, as if holding them might pillow a crash landing. The dark-skinned man turned out to be a renowned chef from Mamounia's, a restaurant known for its exotic delicacies.

In Cuba, while passengers disembarked to safety and filled out endless paperwork, he sat quietly, handwriting the recipe of her favorite Moroccan dish, B'stilla, made from paper thin sheets of buttered phyllo dough, almonds, and chicken soaked and simmered in broth filled with hard to pronounce Middle Eastern spices: coriander, cumin, Za'atar, sumac. Pinches of Aleppo pepper and baharat. Frequenting the restaurant in years to come, she loved sneaking into the kitchen, inhaling the lingering aromas, and reminiscing while he stirred and skewered his signature dishes—all the while gazing at her as if they were still descending from the night sky.

YEARS PASSED. ANCIENT MEMORIES faded and blurred—so much so, she began to wonder if the gypsy had abandoned her, fallen asleep, or taken up residency elsewhere. Deciding to revive her, taking pen to paper, she mapped out a new series of wild dreams: an adventure on the Nile. A train excursion on the Orient Express. A visit to her homeland, Armenia.

DESPITE THE LATENESS OF the hour, a pen threatening to run out of ink, she makes one final journal entry for the world to read:

I will not vanish.

Years will not erase me.

RECALLING A PAIR OF thieves who had soaked cotton balls in chloroform and shoved them into her nostrils, grabbed what few francs she had, then stole her passport, she knew a thing or two about losing one's self, one's identity. Thrown off the train bordering Milan, she had wandered into the dark in search of *gendarmes, della polizia.* A kind stranger appeared from behind the shadows of a rustic building, offering her rescue in broken Italian. She had said yes, later scolded by embassy officials whose stern warnings about trusting strangers were echoed by parents as she wired home for duplicate copies of her passport and traveler's checks. Instead of returning to her dorm, she boarded the next train, a TGV headed for Barcelona. Yearning to run with the bulls, she found her way to a bullfight—gulping sangria beforehand in a dingy café near the YWCA hostel that sheltered her.

SOME STORIES END BADLY, some end well, and others—grow better with time.

SITTING IN SILENCE, BREATHING in the night, a splintered moon casts pieces of shadow onto a slab of cracked, graying cement resting beneath her feet—a reminder that years of wear and tear, underground tremors still reside inside her flesh and bones. A faint invisible aroma—lavender she guesses, dances toward her from the neighbor's patio. Reminiscent of another lifetime, intoxicating to the senses, it prompts, then seduces her to open the ancient journal resting patiently by her side.

Flipping through pages of frayed memories, a card falls from the spine, dusted with glitter and holding promise that *the best is yet to come*. It makes her wonder if there is anything left to salvage of the gypsy whose fading shadow both haunts and hollers while blood still runs through her veins.

AS MORNING DAWNS, SHE jots new entries from a stash of crumpled keepsakes: cocktail napkins, hotel stationery, sticky notes—each surrendering to the ache for more:

Learn Italian
Read Victor Hugo's *Les Misérables* in French
Rent a brownstone in Manhattan
Walk the Camino de Santiago in Spain
See the pyramids

Wilderness Bride

karla k. morton

Written after visiting 62 of all 62 American National Parks

When I was a child,
My parents took me to Arkansas.
We stood inside a church tall and slender
with glass walls that rose high in the woods.

I remember turning to my mother—
how she bent down to catch my whisper:
I want to marry in a place like this.

Since then, I have come to the chapel of redwoods
and rocky shores, traversed deserts,
dog-sled the glaciers,

sojourned caves,
kayaked swamps thick with fireflies,
snorkeled coral reefs beneath the Equator.

I've wept for poisoned lakes, dammed rivers;
the last white wolf;

tasted rainfall in rainforests,
inhaled wild bergamot on tall-grass prairie,
run knee deep with salmon.

I have stepped in muddy prints of Arctic grizzlies,
felt the beating hearts of crocodile,

witnessed terminal snow,
the wild greens of borealis,
smelled the musk of buffalo.

I have come to the chapel 62 times.
I have stood, well-booted,
at the altar of this earth.
I have whispered, every time:
I Do.

Intergenerational

Lila Quinn

Last night I dreamed my mother
cut down the river birch I planted
out front. Paper bark, serrated tear drop
leaves. I cried, cried about time
bursting the truth from inside us, relative
to how long we've kept ourselves small.
With great effort, I breathed through it.
I let her pain inside me
so perhaps we can do it over, a little better
than how it usually goes. We're not supposed to
blame our mothers if we're good feminists,
not supposed to hold her down in our minds,
imagine her surrender and everyone relieved.
There are some places people don't get helped.
Which is why we must try. It must be
fearsome to watch the tree dwarf her, for her
to know any storm might see it ripped away.
I never called her Mama, never read all the labels
of her meds or asked her what her life was like
before her five children. I thought I knew
where the copperheads lived and thorn bushes
cuddled with barbed wire fences around our land.
It's the same with people. So let me do it over.

I know she loved horses. Is that true, Mama?
I know your body ached less, that you made a friend
who's still your friend. I know there's a sweetness stealing
through your ribs and erosion moves the soil,
depleting here, replenishing there.

River Bottom

Molly Akin

My grandmother is a river
A river bottom woman
Soft breasts and wide skirts
Smelling of silt and sun

I remember my grandmother
Like the alchemy of the gulf
The Missouri and the Mississippi
Pouring her life into mine

Because my mother drew from dry wells
It is my father's mother
Who teaches me
To trace a path in water

Where muddy waters
Spill into lightly salted ocean
Our two stories converge
Both gone from home at sixteen

My grandmother and her quilt
Hand-sewn by her mother
Who poured her body
Into scraps of fabric

I keep her quilt on my bedroom chair
Each piece careworn
Passed from hand to hand
Until its star pattern mirrors the sky

I dream of my grandmother
And the keening cry of a bird
Growing louder until it bursts
Washing us in waters no dam can hold

We carry our sorrows
In these fragile vessels
Between wide hips
And river-soaked clothes

My grandmother taught me
To become a river

Weedology and the Wild

Sarah Schiff

HEADING ACROSS CANADA WITH A GIRL I HARDLY KNEW TO A PLACE THAT sounded kooky at best, cultish at worst, felt like a risky move (even for me), but it was all I had. When I'd sailed north from Detroit in a boosted schooner, I'd assumed this new country would have proved refuge enough, but even though they were Great, the Lakes apparently weren't enough distance between me and the memory of what I'd done. I needed somewhere even more remote than this sleepy Canadian town of locks and rapids to disappear into, and Asa, the bartender at the hotel where I'd spent my exiled nights, along with all my cash, happened to know a place.

Plus she had a car.

Once we were out of the Soo, the midnight terrain turned expansive and bare, and Asa slept through the emptiness, her head lolling against the Jeep's floppy window. I didn't like being alone in the quiet dark, so I used the time to rehearse my backstory, something beyond the skeletal tearjerker I'd already used on Asa.

When the sun rose, warming the side of my face, Asa woke and set to picking her cuticles, maybe out of nerves, maybe out of excitement at the prospect of reuniting with her ex-boyfriend.

"Sure you can find this place?" I asked, changing lanes. Trucks trailing jittery boats were converging around us on the highway, and I needed space.

"I'm good with directions." She looked at me as if I'd challenge the statement, and her bright-red eyeshadow practically sent out flames. Then she flicked a strip of flesh onto the floor. "Wouldn't it be wild if Xander could sense me coming?"

"You didn't call ahead?"

"Couldn't. You've got be part of the inner circle to know the phone number."

So. We weren't invited. Asa had described the head of Sovereign Farm as skittish, which meant if Xander didn't want her back, I'd need to find another haven, but something told me this world didn't have many to offer.

The next focus of Asa's nervous energy was her nose ring, which she twisted and slid back and forth through her nostril.

"It looks like you're picking your nose when you do that."

She dropped her hands to her lap. "Do you want me to drive? You haven't gotten a chance to sleep."

"I can't sleep in cars."

In between her commands to turn left or right or go straight, Asa reminisced about her grand romance with Xander. They'd only been dating for several months when he'd dropped out of law school and left Toronto for the wild outskirts of the farm. "He said he was sick of the suited Judases." She tried to make a sound of judgment, but it was devotion.

When we'd glossed over our tragic romantic pasts (mine heavily revised) back at the bar, I'd already liked the sound of this guy. I knew what it was like to be surrounded by traitors.

"The long distance must have been tough," I said now.

"The pretty girl in the next cabin made it tougher."

On a narrow country road, we passed quaint town-centers with quainter tourist shops, then cabins huddled along the many lakes' edges. The roads turned gravelly, with steep climbs and drops, and others were no more than clearings through dense woods.

"Wait," she said, as I righted the Jeep out of a skid.

"What?"

"We shouldn't have come."

"Why not?" She couldn't already be snatching back my chance at sanctuary.

"The last time we saw each other, I called him some terrible things."

"I'm sure he deserved them."

"What if he's still with that girl?"

"You'll win him back."

"How can you be sure?"

"I have no doubt." She looked at me, and I winked.

"There's an old mill over there." Asa pointed beyond some sky-reaching oaks. "You know the kind with those water wheels? When Xander brought me to the farm that one time, we had a picnic lunch there." Her voice caught, then she said, "You can't go in it. The building's all rotted."

When we drove through a ghost town, flattened and dusty, I tried to imagine how it once must have been: bustling with fur-wearing pioneers trading with Natives, going to church in a little wooden chapel, attending school in a drafty wooden house, socializing in the town square, dancing in squares, living in squares.

In front of a fallen-in building was a faded sign promising "Essentials."

As we turned down shaded, sandy trails, branches kept swiping at the Jeep as if trying to hitch a ride. The spruce and fir trees loomed high, blocking the sun. Just when I was wondering if Asa had me completely fooled, that she was actually bringing me out here just so she could eat me in peace, even though having your dinner drive you the whole way and pay for the gas felt rather ill-mannered, we pulled up to a tall steel gate.

"The callbox is new," she said with an exhale. Just from the entry, the place looked more like a billionaire's end-of-world secret bunker than a bunch of stoners' grow-farm. "Should one of us press the call button?"

"My guess is they already know we're here." I looked around for cameras, but they must have been hidden well.

"You're just as nervous as I am," she said, making a try at a laugh, and I hated that she could tell.

As if heading out for a midmorning jog, a man and woman wearing sweats came up the path. Asa and I got out and waited by the Jeep's hood, our arms by our sides, though I felt like we should have raised them in surrender. The air smelled of pencil shavings.

"Can we help you?" the woman asked. She appeared to spend her non-weed-related hours doing bench presses, perhaps lifting the man repeatedly over her head. He was small and trim, as if he'd missed a growth spurt or two. Their hands were empty but their clothes baggy enough to obscure a small arsenal.

I glanced at Asa, who looked as if she was considering getting back into the Jeep and peeling away, leaving me behind forever. "We're here to see Xander," I said.

"How do you know Xander?" the man asked. His voice was surprisingly low-pitched for such a slight man. A man with a voice like that didn't require a big body to compel submission.

Asa opened her mouth then closed it.

"This is Asa Sone. She and Xander used to be close."

"I remember you." The woman put her hand in her pocket. My fingers twitched, even though I was unarmed, but she pulled out a walkie-talkie. "Come in, Xander."

I couldn't hear what the muffled voice on the other end said, but Asa reached for her heart, as if about to pledge allegiance.

"An Asa Sone is here."

There was silence, then the crackled voice again.

"He wants to know what you're doing here." The woman looked bored, as if stuck between children playing telephone.

I was about to answer, but Asa squeaked out, "It's kind of private."

"We're going to need to search you."

"You'll excuse me," the man said in his broadcaster voice when he'd come through the gate. As he patted me down, I was strangely grateful for the feeling of longing, grateful that I could still have that feeling. After what I'd done to Devlin. After what Devlin had done to me.

I shook away the image: *his grinning face hovering above. My tossed purse in the corner.*

Maybe there would be a man for me here too. Someone who would help me forget.

When it was Asa's turn for a once-over, I looked down and found I was standing in cedar chips, the source of the pencil smell. I scraped them away with my boot to the rich black soil underneath.

"To disguise the aroma," the man explained as he rummaged through our bags. "I'm Wally, by the way. That's Valentina. And you are?"

"Sylvie," I said. It was the name I'd given Asa, so it would have to be the one I kept going by, unless the day came when I could get back to being me.

Unless my old life had died with Devlin. Well, where better than a grow-farm to be reborn?

"What's the holdup?" Valentina called from the gate.

Wally held out his hand, an invitation for Asa and me to head down the trail first. Neither he nor Valentina had revealed any weapons, but I considered the possibility that they were marching us to our deaths.

At least it would quiet the guilt.

"I take it Asa is here to rekindle an old love," Wally said from behind us. "Are you moral support?"

"Sylvie's a scientist," Asa said, suddenly having found her voice. "She's looking for a job."

"You'll need to talk to Till then," Wally said.

"Till?"

"The woman in charge, the head, the genius." From the tone of her voice, I imagined Valentina's face making the expression of a googly eyed teenager with a crush.

As we approached a cluster of cabins, the trail turned to open grass, and the smell of cedar gave way to the unmistakable and delicious bite of marijuana. Behind the cabins, I'd soon discover, were five greenhouses, lined up next to each other like rungs on a giant ladder. For now, we entered an A-frame log cabin in the center of the property. Inside, we weaved through the haphazardly situated dining tables, couches, and desks.

"Wait here," Valentina said, indicating armchairs near the fireplace. Stains left by black soot ran like a giant's scratch marks up the wall to the ceiling.

Even though the windows were open, the room was stuffy, and when Valentina left the way we came, Wally caught me eyeing the coffee urn. "Help yourself."

The groan of the front door made me spill some cream. Standing next to Valentina was a woman, tall and willowy, yet fierce in expression, like an egret. She couldn't have been past her mid-thirties, but her hair, styled into a bob that was longer in front, was already paper white. Her jeans were tight-fitting, and she wore a black T-shirt. Minus a ring on her left big toe, her feet were bare.

Wally walked over to her, so she was now flanked by him and Valentina. I concentrated on steadying my hand before taking a sip of coffee, not liking that there was something about Till that made me shake.

"Asa," she said, the disappointment thick in her voice. As Asa stood, she seemed on the verge of saluting. "I thought we'd discussed this."

"Sorry, Till." Asa sounded like an elementary student caught playing a prank. "I just had to see Xander. I couldn't get over how we left things."

"Not only have you returned after I told you not to. You've brought someone else."

"I know you're always looking for good and smart people, and Sylvie's cool."

"I'll determine that for myself," Till said, looking at me for the first time, with no indication of a smile. "Tell it plainly, Asa. Why do you have to see Xander?"

I'd seen her face redden after several drinks back at the bar, but with the shade it turned now, Asa could have been on a weeklong bender. "I love him," she finally got out.

Till crossed her arms. "Wally, arrange a reunion of the love birds."

Xander must have been pining for her. I could see no other reason why she would have let us in.

"Val, Sylvie and I have to talk." Valentina didn't seem to want to leave, but after a warning look in my direction, she too was gone.

Till gestured to an armchair, and she sat on the sofa facing me, bringing her legs up and crossing them. She may as well have been on the cover of a yoga magazine. Or *Couch Digest*.

"Sylvie?" she said, as if waiting for me to correct her. "Tell me about yourself."

Out came my practiced story: I'd grown up smoking with my hippie parents. (True.) I'd then majored in chemistry in college. (Also true. All I'd wanted was to get away from my parents and their life. All I'd wanted was to go straight, blend in, abide by the rules. And look where it had gotten me.) After college, I married a stock trader. (False, as was all that followed, excepting the fact that I had trusted the wrong man.) This husband of mine, whom I called Devlin, dissuaded me from pursuing a career so I could stay home with the kids. When he proved sterile but wouldn't admit it, we spent several years trying to get pregnant, during which time I learned a lot about fertility (a useful bit of knowledge for someone trying to get hired at a grow-farm). When I grew weary of being the test tube rather than working with them, I left. "The divorce was nasty," I said, summoning tears. Devlin resented that I'd made off with 50 percent of his earnings. From his perspective, I'd come to the marriage with virtually nothing and contributed nothing either, even though I'd sacrificed my career for him. His resentment over the alimony soon grew violent. "That's why I came to Canada." Then I showed her the scars on my arms that the real Devlin had left—still shining and pink—and Till's expression released into empathy.

I'd sensed she was the kind of person who considered herself a protector of the woebegone.

If only she knew what I'd really done.

Maybe she would have understood, but I couldn't resist it.

There he was again, his naked belly moist with sweat. My only intent had been to drop off the cash and leave. Why couldn't it have been enough for him?

Till's throat-clearing brought me back from my memories. "Xander hasn't been the same since Asa left. I'll give you both a month to prove you can earn your keep. Lord knows we can use the extra hands."

"Business good?"

"Almost too good." When she smiled, tiny wrinkles edged around her eyes. Her pride for the place was in those wrinkles. "Lorelei's roommate took off a couple months ago, so you can move in with her." At the mention of a defector, her tone had changed to bitterness.

On our way to my new cabin, Wally gave me a tour of Sovereign Farm—the greenhouses, gardens, vineyard, chickencoop, the barn that housed dairy cows and goats—while asking what I already knew about the doomed, but maybe resurrecting, romance between Asa and Xander. The tale, which had apparently taken on mythic proportion at the farm, went that the woman Xander cheated on Asa with was also hooking up with someone else. When she got pregnant, apparently by the other guy, they had to leave, since children weren't allowed on the premises. I was glad to hear the other woman was no longer around. For Asa's sake.

The cabins at the front of the property, which were newer and bigger, were the homes of the more established crewmembers, "the inner circle" Asa had mentioned. The cabins in back, where the salespeople, trimmers, and packers lived, were the originals from when Sovereign Farm was founded by Till's mother. Hazel, it turned out, had written the book considered the Bible of cannabis cultivation.

As I crossed the threshold into my new home, a soothing feeling came over me, a release of the muscles I'd been clenching since leaving Devlin's apartment back in Detroit.

Even though there should have been no question about who was the one with the power. So what if Devlin had discovered my breaking of an archaic rule, its intent to keep old men from taking advantage of their secretaries back before women were even allowed to reach the kind of position I had. It wasn't meant for someone like me, someone who'd simply followed her natural feelings to—

someone who was technically off-limits

someone who happened to be Devlin's coworker

worse: his roommate.

How could I have known that my new, young, enthusiastic lover's confidant was the jealous, blackmailing, embittered type?

How could I have known that he'd wanted more than my job, more than my savings, more than my power, more than I could give him?

Then came Wally's voice, warm and deep. "Lorelei's still on duty. I'll leave you to get settled."

That's when Asa came through the door with a beautiful man at her side and a maniacal grin on her face.

"I hear I have you to thank for bringing her back," Xander said as he came in for a hug, holding me tight before returning, too soon, to Asa's arms.

The emotion I tried to feel in the moment was joy—joy for Asa—but my head was blazing as if I'd sucked down a gallon of ice cream. It meant trouble: there's only one way for the burn of envy to thaw.

I'd found a place that felt like it was made for someone in just my situation, but if I wasn't going to screw it up and do something (well, another thing) that most people would probably call terrible, I knew I had to find a man of my own. Unfortunately, at least half of Sovereign Farm's men were Hazel's original crew, and there seemed to be a generously high tolerance for sloppiness—stained teeth, mangy hair, overgrown toenails.

I couldn't figure out if I was attracted to Xander because there was actually something about him or because he was someone to be competed for. How easily the desired became the desirable.

He was almost always hiplocked with Asa, but because of their difference in height, they appeared like lopsided conjoined twins. When she came in for a hug, he had to prep himself, bend down almost to a squat.

I would be a better fit.

Asa had stopped wearing her eyeshadow, conforming to the unspoken dictum here that makeup, leather clothing, high heels—anything that looked like effort or needless animal sacrifice—was taboo. Though Wally and Valentina, Sovereign's security team, had been pretty intense, the rest of Sovereign's employees went through their days with an open placidity. They lived and played where they worked. The trimmers would sit hunched over buds for eight hours, clipping away in their surgical gloves as if in a hypnotic state. The packers gathered the manicured nuggets and sealed them in labeled airtight jars, noting on clipboards the weights and values. Even if the work didn't require much brain activity, handling the plants demanded a delicate touch, so few of the crewmembers smoked on duty. They enjoyed the fruits of their labor when the working day was done. Sometimes they'd unfurl their bodies on yoga mats under the trees or nap in braided hammocks. Other times, it got pretty weird, but I tried not to judge. If we occasionally had to participate in snot-rattling sharing sessions ("hello, my name is" crap) or perform a highly choreographed dance (with extra emphasis on the hip thrusts) to thank the nature gods for an especially fruitful harvest, so be it. I knew from experience that, in the real world, people like them, people who don't bend their wills to the demands of invisible conventions, usually end up controlled or silenced or expelled. I'd once been on the other side, but now I was among their ranks. Right where I belonged.

Since his breakup with Asa, Xander had been promoted to Sovereign Farm's business manager and therefore had entered the inner circle. Even if incomplete, his law training allowed him to draw up contracts with the dispensary owners that looked and sounded official, though they wouldn't have held up in any court. At least not yet.

When Asa was assigned to accompany a salesman on his delivery route, she and Xander had to detach themselves. It was clear he worried about her on the road with Boots, a man fifteen years her senior but undeniably charming to some—one of those "wait'll you hear this" guys. I wondered if Till was testing them.

She was definitely testing me by making me a trimmer, the menial work. Despite my lab experience in college, I kept slicing through the surgical gloves, my skin torn up and bloody by the end of each day. When the weather was mild, Till would join me on the picnic bench while I pruned the colas. My real post-college work as a pharmaceutical consultant would have been immediate cause for expulsion, but it sure came in handy now as I impressed her with my knowledge of genetic splicing, the long-suppressed benefits of medical marijuana, and the drug war. In turn, she taught me about the cultural histories of cannabis use and harvesting, her growing heroes, and the best strategies for managing pH levels. I didn't even know the cannabis plant had separate sexes—turned out the female plants produced what you wanted to smoke, and the males were pretty much just there for the seeds.

Uncanny the similarities.

Till's voice was low and wispy, like steam from a freshly baked pie, yet she spoke with such assuredness and eloquence—I wondered how she wasn't already a world leader.

When she left, always too soon, my cabin-mate Lorelei would bring her pile of buds over and tease me about all the blood on my gloves, calling me Edward Stonerhands. Braless, with frizzy salt and pepper braids, Lorelei loved to fill me in on who was dating or broken up, who was just screwing, whose love was unrequited, who secretly hated whom, who openly hated whom. What else of intrigue was there between humans, after all, besides love and hate?

Lorelei's favorite scandals were about the tumbles of inner circle members into the outer circle's beds, which never lasted long, and that set me wondering about the chances of survival for Xander and Asa.

"How do you get into the inner circle?" I asked.

"Apparently you have to do something pretty out there, but the payoff is huge."

In the three years she'd been at Sovereign Farm, Lorelei had overheard enough to figure out a semblance of its origin story. When Hazel founded it, Till was still in the womb, and there was ongoing speculation about which of the older men on the place was her father, if any. No one had dared ask Hazel, and no one would dare ask Till now, if she even knew. "It's possible Hazel didn't know herself," Lorelei said.

It wasn't long after Lorelei arrived that Hazel, who'd been suffering from ALS, died. When she could no longer smoke—her lips unable to form a bond, her lungs too weak to inhale deeply—she moved to a cannabis tea, but eventually sipping and swallowing proved beyond her as well. Since injection didn't work for cannabis, Hazel was robbed of the one treatment that had provided comfort, the cure-all she'd devoted her life to. Through gestures and scribbles, she'd asked Till to kill her.

Which she did.

Which meant both of us had blood on our hands.

* * *

WHEN TILL PROMOTED ME to the greenhouses, it came with a huge relief. Despite the security I felt here, I'd already started growing restless. Sometimes I found myself fantasizing about my own farm. Or maybe taking over this one as Till's heir. Before Devlin had stolen it away from me, I'd been well on my way to a life of self-sufficiency and professional respect. I wanted it back. I wanted to be my own boss again, to lord over an army of workers, to feel accomplished and productive, but maybe this time with a crown of marijuana leaves instead of a suit. If Devlin had let me, I would have kept wearing that suit, even though in it, I couldn't reach my arms over my head. Here, I was free.

Soon I took on a research project: an analysis of the molecules in our plants so we could track the levels of THC, CBD, ocimene, nerolidol, pinene—all the intermixed chemicals that produced cannabis's inscrutable benefits. Surrounded by petri dishes and microscopes, I was brought back to my college days. If my findings worked out, we'd be able to provide documentation that our products were of the highest quality as well as offer select strains for highly specified purposes.

And not only that. Till pointed out that the work I was doing was noble, humanitarian even. While the government was solely invested in studying marijuana to prove its detriments, it conveniently ignored that the wild weed had been providing peace and healing to people across the globe for millennia.

If this didn't get me into the inner circle, I didn't know what would.

One afternoon when I was checking some mature plants for mites, I heard crinkling footsteps behind me on the white mylar, then that grungy, tender voice I'd come to love, despite myself. "How's the lady with the closed mouth and green thumb?"

"That must be the gentleman with the strong arms and discerning eye."

He laughed, and when I pulled away from the magnifying scope, I had to blink to see him clearly. In the fragrant heat of the greenhouse, he unzipped his hoodie and wrapped it around his waist, revealing a white tank stretched across his lean build.

"No complaints here," I said, returning my gaze to the scope. A tiny mite skittered across a leaf, so I squeezed it dead between my fingers then dug some hand sanitizer out from my apron pocket and rubbed in into my hands, the required protocol after touching a pest. When I shifted down the line, Xander followed, fingering the leaves. "You shouldn't do that," I said, layering my voice with a tease. "You'll stress them out."

"You really think plants experience anxiety?"

Was this him confiding in me? "Aren't you the heretic. Till sure thinks so."

He sighed, and with that sigh, I knew why he'd come to me, an assumed ally of the burdened Asa and Xander relationship.

If he was pining for her because she was out on the Canadian roads with Boots, it was only more proof that relativity was the rule when it came to our longing for others.

Beyond wordplay, there have been moments—a flick of hair here, a close dance there—when I could have sworn something was connecting us. Unless it was all just to make Asa jealous.

Over a shared joint, I let him talk about her. She'd repeatedly forgiven him for cheating, but still he worried Asa wanted to get even with him, maybe only subconsciously. And he wanted her to have an assignment here on the farm, with him, but Till wouldn't allow it—Asa didn't have the required skills or education. At every opportunity, it seemed, Till wanted to remind Xander that Asa shouldn't have come at all. "Sometimes—" he said, holding in a big pull, and I watched, curious if he'd say something negative about Till. I'd already noticed inner-circle members cutting off their conversations at my approach, which made me wonder if people here weren't as content as they seemed.

A striped brown wolf spider high-stepped along the edge of the table, and I was tempted to flatten it too, but spiders help with pest control, so I let it be.

When Xavier finally released the thick plume, "never mind" whiffed out in the midst of it. He wiped some sweat from his brow with the bottom of his shirt, and I couldn't help counting his abs. He grinned when he caught me.

After he'd stubbed out the joint in a bucket of mulch, he said, "Thanks for the talk," and his walk away was a subtle swagger. If I hadn't been stoned and confused, I might have chased after him, grabbed him from behind, and made him forget all about Asa. As it was, though, my feet remained stuck to the crackling white floor.

IT WASN'T LONG AFTER that when Till surprised me in the same greenhouse where Xander had come for comfort. "You're being initiated tonight. This is your opportunity to prove your loyalty to Sovereign Farm. And to me."

I cleared my throat to thank her, shocked at how much it meant to be embraced and officially welcomed by a place where I still wasn't sure I wanted to stay. But maybe this would change things, along with my prospects. What could I accomplish now? With whom by my side?

Before leaving, Till winked at me, but it was a solemn wink, like a broken baby doll's.

After dinner, most of the crew were in various states of repose in the central cabin, smoking and chatting and rubbing their bellies, but I couldn't relax; I kept catching glances from the older crewmembers, especially Kimi, Till's godmother and Sovereign's unofficial second-in-command.

Then I felt a tap on my shoulder. "Come with me," Till said, and Lorelei shot me a peace sign.

I'd never been inside Till's cabin before. She was the only one of us who lived alone. After I took a seat in a rocking chair by the fire, the only source of light, she went to the kitchenette to make me some special tea. "My mom's specialty," she said, barely giggling at the pun. Then she sounded a sorrow so deep and shuddering I wondered if I should go over, hold her or pat her back. But she didn't seem like the kind of person who wanted to be touched.

I'd never known her to be with another person romantically, had never even seen her flirt, and people called her a nun behind her back. Where did she find companionship? I tried to glance down the hall toward the bedrooms but couldn't see anything through the darkness. Maybe there was a library of books that she was slowly working her way through. Or she had a contraband television. I almost started laughing out loud when I imagined an S&M chamber back there.

Everyone has their secrets, which meant it wasn't impossible that Xander carried one about me.

When the kettle whistled, Till brought over a mug. The flickers of the fireplace highlighted the gray pouches beneath her eyes, as if her irises were leaking and pooling beneath her skin. The whole illusion was so overwhelming, I nearly blurted out an excuse to leave. Up until now, I'd always trusted Till; she seemed to go through life armed with the unequivocal knowledge that she was living as the world or fate or God or some other supreme source intended her to. Or, at the very least, it was what she wanted for herself. I envied her that.

The tea she held out to me was yellowy and appeared weak. "What's in it?" I asked.

"Something that strengthens the tenuous connection between body and mind."

If she'd been anyone else, I'd have told her my preferred drink was tequila, but I have to admit I was curious and craved her validation. What else could explain my willingness to take it, after having once been on the other side?

The tea tasted how freshly mown grass smells. "Aren't you going to join me?"

"I've already had mine," and she proceeded to explain the secret tradition her mother had established, known only to the inner circle.

"Blood, sweat, and tears go into the creation of these wonderworking plants. All that makes us *us*. They *are* us, and we are them. Government, society, institutions reject what we stand for. But individuals rely on us. We live in the dark so others can be themselves in the light." Part of me wanted to laugh at the ceremoniousness, as if she were about to shoot me off to an undiscovered planet. Then I remembered what she'd said about the nobility of our work—its necessary defiance. Maybe it was the drink, but her words soon took on three-dimensionality, hovering in the air like party balloons. I had a purpose, she was telling me. I served others. I did good.

All I had to do was believe it.

"You sweat from the labor in the cloudy warmth of the greenhouse. You bleed when you cut yourself trimming." Part of me then wondered if I was about to go through some kind of blood-spilling ritual. It must have been the tea that didn't send me running at the thought. "You cry when the past's emotional lurchings become unbearable." I assumed that was a reference to the insufferable group therapy sessions that I always got stoned for and never contributed to. As much as I cared for and trusted these people, there was no way they could have my story. Even in a place like this, there was no way to tell it. It was hard to be considered taboo here, but, unlike Till's, mine was not a mercy kill.

Unless I could make myself believe it.

"Your purpose tonight is to forge a permanent bond with the farm. First, I need you to select a member of the inner circle who will serve as witness, ensure your safety, and be there as a source of bodily comfort should you request it."

I wondered what she meant by *bodily comfort* but didn't ask. I'd find out soon enough.

Her face floated above as she listed my options: all the older men and women; a couple younger growers; Wally and Valentina. Not Lorelei or Asa. None of the salespeople or trimmers. When she said *Xander*, I nodded. Since Till rarely smiled, I couldn't be sure if that slight rise of one side of her mouth meant she approved of my choice.

She unclipped the walkie-talkie from her belt and called for him.

Then, with the tea warming me from the inside, I followed her down the hallway, concentrating on each footfall because the floor seemed to have sunk beneath the surface of the earth. In the last room was a twin bed, topped with a hand-woven quilt, and Till puffed the pillow as if she were about to lie down. In the corner was a wheelchair, empty and gleaming, as though the black nylon seat were regularly polished. I stared at a silver urn on a small wooden desk until I heard footsteps. Xander leaned against the door jamb, a pose I could tell, even in my state, was to camouflage the nerves. "Ready?" he said to me.

The tea made it impossible to stop grinning at his beauty. "Where did you come from?" I said, and he blushed. Devlin's face crept into my head then, but I shook it away. *Damn your interference. Damn the way you looked at me. Damn you that the money wasn't enough.*

I hadn't been to the woods behind the property before, but I knew dogs roamed the place, guarding against intruders. Sturdy viburnum trees had been planted beyond the cedar chips, emitting their spicy scent as an additional cover for any escaping cannabis odors. There was something masculine about the smell, and I walked closer to Xander, who carried a hiking pack over his layers and lit our path with a propane lantern. Still, the darkness seemed to cast a shadow, a darker outline of the darkness of night, and even beneath my ankle-length down coat and wool hat, I shivered. Or was it my skin humming?

"When do I get to know what's going on?" I asked.

"This is my first time," he whispered, almost before I'd finished talking, as if it was a heavier burden than the pack.

"First time?"

"I went through my own initiation, but this is the first I've . . . overseen." I couldn't tell if that was excitement or something else in his voice. The skin-humming was growing stronger, especially between my legs. It felt like all I had to do was keep walking, and soon I'd be satisfied.

"Till said it involves proving my loyalty through blood, sweat, and tears?"

"You've already done that. When Hazel welcomed each crewmember to the inner circle, the sign of their returned devotion and commitment to the cause of new growth was, uh, the release of a fourth fluid." In that *uh* was all his embarrassment. "So, this is actually a . . ."

Loving his modesty, I realized he wanted me to finish the thought. "Fertility ritual?"

"Are you okay with that?"

"Do I have a choice?"

"Not if you want to stay." His laugh seemed to emit a question mark into the frigid air. "When Hazel died, Till reformed the tradition. She wanted to give crew members the opportunity to consent, to select their witness. And now you have the choice to—" He patted his pocket as if he'd forgotten something. "To make the offering by yourself, or I can assist. Either way, both of us serve as witness."

"Both of you?"

Xander pointed his thumb toward the backpack. "I've got her in here."

"Who?"

His sigh seemed to join the question mark still following us through the air. "Till believes her mother was so powerful a presence, so deeply connected to the land, that there's no way she's fully gone." As if purifying our path, tiny snowflakes fell before us. I felt them catching in my lashes and tried to blink them away, but they thickened and iced there, as if I was on my way to becoming a snowwoman. The humming seemed to have transferred to the air now, making it hard for me to think beyond it, my entire being dissipating into its realm. Dimly, somewhere in a quiet space beyond the humming, I was aware that everything Xander was saying was fucking insane.

When we reached a clearing, the moon's beams filtered through the low-hanging clouds, and I gave up on blinking the snowflakes away. They seemed to be my essence.

Then Xander called my name, and I looked back to find he'd assembled a small tent and built a fire. The flames kissed my gloves, and the contrast of the heat and cold scattered the buzzing in my skin. What if I stepped into the fire and turned into a deer? Then the cannibalistic worries returned. Was Xander going to eat me?

I stared at the fire until a face appeared in it. But it wasn't mine. It was Devlin's. Burning. Right where he belonged. Right where he'd forced me to send him.

Those pills had been meant for my own protection, that's why they were in my purse—just one into a creeper's drink for a quiet night at the bar. How gullible—to believe six was the recommended dose.

The snowwoman I'd become breathed, and my iciness overcame his flames.

IN THE TENT, XANDER and I sat cross-legged, waiting for our bodies to warm the space. I'd tried to deny it, but here was the man I needed, right beside me.

He unzipped my coat and put his arm around me. Pulled together as a constellation, he was a star in space and I another.

But there they were—two Hazels, one in her urn and one in a framed photograph. At first I thought the face was Till's; they looked so much alike.

"Can we put a blanket down?" I asked. My upper body had warmed with Xander's contact, but my bottom half felt chilled from the ground.

"You can't lose touch with the earth. That's what, or who, you're connecting with. Giving yourself to. That's the bond. That's what'll allow Sovereign Farm and all of us living on it to continue thriving." It sounded like he had to remind himself of the lines.

Though I had no intention of stopping him, I couldn't look away from Hazel's face. I almost kicked at the picture but feared toppling the urn next to it. Spilling Hazel probably wouldn't be the best way to prove my loyalty to Till.

If that's what I was even doing here in this tent.

Then, unbidden, Asa's face appeared, a companion for the Hazels, all of them now my witnesses.

If I didn't ask it, I knew she wouldn't leave: "Does Asa know you're here?"

"No." He swallowed but didn't stop rubbing. "No one can know about the initiation until they've gone through it."

"So one day you'll tell her?"

He took off his toque and fluffed his hair. "Asa will never be in the inner circle."

I almost asked why, but I knew. Till didn't like her. Or at least didn't like her with Xander. Would she like me better? "Who did you bring for your initiation?"

"Till."

Jealousy filled my heart like an injection. "I didn't know she was an option."

"She doesn't want to be the mandated choice."

I shook my head, unappeased. "She didn't list her name." Or had I responded too eagerly when she'd come to Xander's? Like a chess piece, a rueful feeling displaced the jealousy. Had I missed the chance to set myself up for greater reward?

Xander was wiser than I.

When he asked, "Do you regret your selection?" I feared my thoughts had decamped from my head, but then I looked at his face, the jawline that conveyed confidence and sensitivity at once, this man I'd been admiring before I even met him, this capable, loving specimen.

Here I was, in the middle of a winter forest, beyond conscious concerns. I might as well have been in another dimension, in someone else's reality where I was just the affable guest.

I made my choice and, with Xander's gentle help, gave myself to the earth, hoping desperately that it would keep on giving to me.

FOR TWO MONTHS, I wondered what that night had made of us, although I wasn't sure if I was avoiding Xander or he was avoiding me. Until, that is, he showed up late at my new upgraded, inner-circle cabin. "Are they asleep?" he asked through fast-coming breaths. My new roommates, he meant: Valentina, of the constant devotion to Till, and Kimi, Till's enigmatic godmother.

When I nodded, Xander sat and rubbed his hands before the fireplace. "It's Asa," he whispered once he'd caught his breath.

Great, I thought. "What about her?"

He shook his head. "I'm not sure I'm supposed to say."

"Then why are you here?"

"I have to tell somebody," he said.

"You seem angry."

"I am." He said it like a revelation.

"Did you tell Asa about . . . our night?"

"No," he said with a start. "You didn't, did you?"

"Of course not." What was more worrisome: Asa learning about us, or Till learning I'd broken confidentiality?

"Why do I even care anymore?" he asked, but more to himself.

Earlier that day, he went on to explain, he'd gone looking for Asa. She wasn't anywhere—in her cabin, the main hall, the barn, or even the greenhouses, which were off-limits to her anyway, and none of the trucks were missing from the lot. Spiked by jealousy, he'd visited Boots' cabin. After a couple more worrying hours, he searched all of them, including mine, though I'd been out, splicing clones. So he'd asked Kimi, who suggested with an odd tone in her voice that he check Till's cabin. But people never went knocking on her door; you were summoned. He forced himself to wait another hour before he couldn't anymore, and when no one answered his knock, he let himself in, something only to be done in case of emergency. By this point, though, it had taken on emergency status. If Asa wasn't in there, she'd been grabbed up by wolves.

As he spoke these forbidden words, Xander kept checking behind him for Kimi and Valentina, and I concentrated on expressing concern instead of begrudging how distraught he was over the absent Asa. A small part of me hoped she'd gone the way of Little Red Riding Hood.

But there they were, in the same room where he'd picked me up for my initiation. Slumped in the gleaming wheelchair was Asa, her head on one shoulder, with the silver urn between her legs. Till was talking in an unnaturally high-pitched voice. The only words Xander caught were "made me" before a sound of horror escaped his throat. She screamed at him to get out, and he sprinted to his cabin, shaking and distressed. Should he go back and rescue Asa? But from what? What was that even?

Not long after, Till came knocking on his door with anguish and an explanation.

"She was trying to reconnect with her mother," Xander said now, disgust in his voice. Shortly after Hazel's death, Till began inviting an outer-circle crewmember to her cabin for monthly visits. The first one selected had disappeared without warning five years ago. Then it was Lorelei's roommate, who, I remembered, had left shortly before we arrived. "She gives them a tea that makes them forget basically everything. They just think they've been invited to the boss's cabin for an intimate talk. But those previous two must have figured out something was off and gotten the hell out of here. I mean, I always knew Till was eccentric, but I never would have thought—"

Even commanders need someone to confide in was the startling explanation that came to my mind before wondering if Till's drug of choice was the same I'd once kept in my purse. The same that, on a false promise of longer performance, Devlin had overused. The same that had saved me.

When Xander grabbed my hands in his, strong but trembling, I rubbed my thumbs over the dancing ridges on the backs of his hands. "What are we supposed to do?" he asked.

Till had taken unsuspecting employees and used them for her own needs, something powerful people have been doing since the beginning. And relatively speaking, what she was doing was pretty benign. Was it any weirder than the initiation I'd been through? Than this whole place I'd been calling home?

I was no one to judge, but this might have been just the catalyst I needed. Despite all I'd learned, despite the protection of the farm, despite my admission to the inner circle, despite even the fantastic hope of one day having Xander for myself, Sovereign was revealing itself as too small, *too* remote. Yes, those were the qualities that had brought me here, but what did it mean to rise in the ranks in a place like this? And how far could I ultimately go? Always, Sovereign Farm would be Till's.

I could have told Xander he had no reason to be upset. And it wasn't like Asa had much agency in the situation, so she couldn't be blamed. Till commanded, and we obeyed. Besides, he'd done far worse.

But now with my path before me, I kept all that to myself. "I understand your feelings."

"Maybe I'm being hypocritical," he said, evidently realizing what I had. "But she's so young. Impressionable."

"You must have cheated on her for a reason."

"But somehow this feels worse. It's like she's—"

"Tainted?" I finished for him, although I didn't know which "she" either of us was talking about.

"Yes!" he looked into my eyes as if I was the lone person on earth who understood him. "I mean, shit. Till thinks the cause of Hazel's ALS was being exposed to too much carbon dioxide before the greenhouses had sufficient ventilation systems." He guffawed. I kept to myself that that seemed to be the least of her magical thinking.

But there was no need for magical thinking to become someone like Till, powerful and in charge, no longer the one commanded, no longer vulnerable. I'd gotten what I'd needed out of this isolated, dirty, strange, strange place. Time enough had passed. No one had come looking for me. And I'd been reading the news.

With knowledge and experience and a restored resolve, it was time to get back to the world.

"Have you seen the latest polls?" I asked.

With every passing month, more and more Americans were supporting legalization. To many people's surprise, it was looking like it would happen there before Canada, at least in some places, including Xander's home state of Washington. His grin was like a ticket to freedom.

And the Washington woods were even farther from Detroit than here.

As WE PRIVATELY MADE our arrangements to leave, Xander and I publicly became a couple. Asa accosted me over breakfast one morning, calling me a skank, cheater, traitor. Then she slapped me across the face, and I focused on the burn. The rest of the crewmembers just sipped coffee and poured their syrup. No doubt they'd witnessed similar scenes before. Sucking down my humiliation, I let her tire herself out, and when she cried, I let my own tears come. Maybe I was sad about losing a friend, even though we hadn't been that close. But we'd come to this place together, and soon I'd be leaving it behind. With the man who'd brought both of us here.

It wasn't long before she was roaming the grounds arm-in-arm with Boots. I tried to distract Xander from the image and worried his aspersions against them were a displacement for lingering feelings for her. If so, I told myself they'd dissipate once we were back across the border.

The night we left, we gathered essentials: canned foods, bedding, gas, and, the most precious of all, several dozen cannabis seeds. Together they were worth thousands of dollars. Since we were taking Till's babies, which she would have trademarked if she could have, we needed to get far out of her reach, and quick. The loss of those seeds would mean more to her than the loss of us.

Once Wally, on night patrol, had made his way to the forest's edge in the back of the property, we drove Boots' truck out the gate and into our new futures.

Chased away by a man whose inflated self-estimation had made him vulnerable to a woman who always found a way out, I had left my old life in Detroit, along with my heart. But I felt it again in the Canadian wild, and now I knew it could beat anything back.

The Lunar Light Within

Jess Whetsel

I am learning
to see myself
as the moon
To honor my phases
of light and shadow
To dance to the cadence
of the song within me
To surrender to the cycle
of blood and creation
spontaneous combustion
and rebirth within the flames
I am learning
to see myself
as the moon
Always whole
even when I only
show the part of myself
that is luminous
The part of me that believes
I will get through this
The part of me that trusts
in the silent rhythms
that guided generations

of ancestors before me
I am learning
to see myself
as the moon
Perfect because of
my imperfections
not despite them
the bumps and craters
on the surface
the topographical map
of my life
each rise and fall
a daily reminder
that I am still breathing
I am learning
to see myself
as the moon
Even when the night sky
envelops me in black velvet
and I am caught in the currents
of my spiraling mind
I tread water until the sunlight
stretches over the horizon
and a sliver of me shines through
to light my way back home

The Day She Decided to Wear No Clothes

Joanna Zarkadas

The day she decided to wear no clothes
Was a special day
That required special attention
She woke early
To the sound of bird songs
The bluest sky
And a soft October wind

From her jewelry box she gathered
Her thirteen necklaces
The pendants, the chains, the beads
And the extra long one
Of rainbow fabric balls
That made three loops around her neck
The combination hung heavy
Between her bare breasts

Next she grabbed her seven bracelets
The one of moon and stars
The lotus flower
The two plain silver bands

The three of various colored beads
And arranged four on her left wrist
The rest on her right one

She covered all her fingers with rings
Surprising herself with how many
She had collected over a lifetime
But seldom bothered to wear
When she ran out of fingers
She placed them on her toes
Loving the happy tapping sound
They made each time
She walked across the kitchen tiles

From her closet she took her seventeen scarves
The five thinnest she wound around her head
Hippy style across her forehead
Knotted at the back with tails of varying length
Hanging down her back
Each of the other twelve
She looped once through the five bands
Creating multicolored cloth hair
That swayed and bounced
When she walked

Once she had finished accessorizing herself
She got out her collection of Sharpies
Twenty-four different colors
Of varying widths
These she used to draw colorful rings
Around each of her free hanging breasts
And one hip-to-hip rainbow

That traversed across her stomach
Her sparse grey pubic hair
Was turned into grass
That sprouted a row of red tulips

Next, with her right hand
She drew thick red stripes down each of her legs
To honor the menstrual blood that used to flow freely
Then a series of rainbow polk-a-dots on her left arm
With her left hand
She drew small irregular shaped circles
On her right arm

Once she was fully decorated
She sat at the piano
To play the three songs
She could play with both hands
From memory
Moon River by Henry Mancini
Where Is Love by Lionel Bart
And Edelweiss by Richard Rodgers

After her concert
She walked out to the back deck
To feel the afternoon sun
And warm wind
On her bare skin
Not caring if anyone saw her
In her birthday suit
Though no one did

Feeling satisfied with her day
She came inside
Set up her tripod
And took one photo
To mark the day
She began her walk
Towards seventy-seven

Contributors

AMY SOSCIA earned her MFA in writing from Albertus Magnus College. Her writing has been published in *The Year's Best Dog Stories* (2021), *Fredericksburg Literary & Arts Review, One Hundred Voices* Vol. II, *Down in the Dirt Magazine*, the *Westie Imprint, 898 Literary Journal*, and *Chicken Soup for the Soul: Recovering from Brain Injuries*. She lives in Maryland with her husband Paul and their three West Highland white terriers (Tucker, Walter McRuffian, and Lily). Her forthcoming debut novel is titled *The Frozen Game*. Learn more at www.amysoscia.com.

MIA CARA KINSELLA is an English major at UC Irvine, competitive female bikini bodybuilder, actress, and singer/songwriter from Orange County, California. In her poem, "Confession of a Female Bodybuilder," Mia Cara stresses acceptance and empowerment for women in the gym. She touches on the different reactions she has experienced in response to wanting to build muscle and societal views on women being in an environment traditionally seen as "masculine." Mia Cara believes that creative expression is the key to altering perceptions, and she plans to continue pursuing this through writing.

KAYLA AGNIR is an Appalachian Trail thru-hiker with a lifelong passion for writing poetry and prose, drawing inspiration from nature and life experiences. She works as an occupational therapy practitioner for a public school system, and lives in Massachusetts with her partner, two dogs, and two snakes.

DON CARTER is a writer, sommelier, wine retailer, and educator living in the suburbs of northern New Jersey. His writing platform is called WineSnark: The Wise-Ass Guide to Wine Appreciation, but in recent years he has ventured out of his wine writing comfort zone and turned to writing memoir. The jury is still out on his new attempts at fiction writing. You can find Don's work at Winesnark.com.

AURORA BONES currently teaches English at a University in Illinois. She earned her MA from Southern Illinois University at Edwardsville, and an MFA from Naropa University in Boulder, Colorado. When she isn't reading or writing she enjoys learning to play the ukulele, planting sunflowers, and hiking in aspen forests. She often spends her evenings catching fireflies and then letting them go.

HEATHER MURRAY is a writer and librarian from the forests of New England. Her nonfiction pieces have been published with Stampington & Company magazines and her ghost story "Lily and the Spectre" was recently included in a short story anthology published by the Mark Twain House in collaboration with the Bushnell Theater. She is currently working on an adult fantasy novel.

KATHERINE ROYCE is an emerging author from Western Australia. She tries valiantly to get teenagers enthused about English, and is relentlessly bullied by her horses, cats, and chickens.

LAUREL MAXWELL is a poet from Santa Cruz, California, whose work is inspired by life's mundane and the natural world (especially the ocean). Her work has appeared in baseballballard.com, *coffecontrails*, *phren-z*, and *Verse-Virtual*. When not writing Laurel enjoys putting her feet in the sand, reading, traveling, and trying not to make too much of a mess baking in a too-small kitchen.

DIANE ALLERDYCE serves as associate dean and chair of humanities and culture for the PhD program in interdisciplinary studies at Union Institute and University, where she's taught since 2008. She was the cofounder and chief academic officer of Toussaint L'Ouverture High School for Arts and Social Justice, a Florida charter school serving mostly immigrant students from the Caribbean, from its founding in 2001 until closing in 2022. She also developed and directed Teaching by Heart, a teacher-training program in Haiti, from 2009 through 2019. In addition to several individual poems, her creative publications include a chapbook, *Whatever It Is I Was Giving Up* (Pudding House, 2007), and *House of Aching Beauty* (Editions Perle des Antilles, 2012). Her story "The Gift" appeared in the *North American Review* (Fall 2019) and was inspired in part by Wallace Stegner's "Goin' to Town"; an interview about her process appears at northamericanreview.org/open-space /conversation-diane-allerdyce-discusses-her-story-gift-her-partner-rory-spearing. More recently, her short story "Kochma" appeared in TulipTree's *Stories That Need to Be Told 2022*; it was also first-place winner in the UK-based National Association of Writers and Groups (NAWG)'s 2022 Open Competition for Fiction and was republished with permission in their *2022 Anthology of Award-Winning Writing*.

JOANNE GRAM is a queer woman with a master's degree, living and writing poetry in Lansing, Michigan. Joanne is intrigued by lives past and future but is disgusted by the rampant injustice in her current time and space. For many years, Joanne wrote and presented research papers on improving public administration for the International Conference on Public Administration. More recently, she finds the medium of poetry, written and spoken, a more satisfying method for making her various statements. Her poems appear in a variety of publications, including *Of Rust and Glass, Writing in a Woman's Voice, Peninsula Poets*, and the annual poetry publication of the East Lansing Arts Festival.

J. MICHELE MOLL, a New Orleans native, has been working on getting older since birth. She is quite proud of how far she's come in her goal to continue getting older on a daily basis and, in fact, has been successful so far—to the immense bewilderment and slack-jawed astonishment of friends, acquaintances, every one of her ex-husbands, the well-meaning folks she met in rehab, the other drivers she passes on her daily commute, and the strenuous and well-funded efforts of the cosmetics and anti-aging industrial complex. Her motto is don't stop breathing and so far, it's working.

Raised in Honolulu, MARGARET SPECK OGAWA is a biracial writer (American Japanese/Irish/German/French), with past careers in marketing, product management, and fashion. She resides in the Seattle area, is currently working on her master's degree in creative writing and literature from Harvard University, and is a member of the Pacific Northwest Writers Association. In her wildest dreams, she travels to all the world capitals and stays long enough to absorb the variety of cultures and write a story within each. Her recent publishing history includes the poem "Butter and Shoyu," about the frustration of having to check the "other" box on forms asking for personal data. It was published on the Mixed Asian Media website in February 2023 (mixedasianmedia.com/butter-and-shoyu).

HANNAH HINDLEY is a wilderness guide and essayist with an MFA from the University of Arizona. She is the recipient of the Barry Lopez Prize, the Thomas Wood Award in Journalism, and a Carson Scholarship in science communication. Find her work at hannahhindley.com.

Hailing from Canton, Ohio, award-winning author M. KATE ALLEN has made her way to Cleveland, Berlin, central Minnesota, the San Francisco Bay Area, and beyond in search of unusual story seeds that she can nurture into full bloom. She is a fan of places where history and memory are well-tended, and she especially enjoys reading/writing about places as characters. As a feminist seeking intersectionality and as a proud member of the LGBTQ+ community, Kate is always on the lookout for gaps in cultural metanarratives that are big enough for one's entire, messy, curious, intuitive, brave, authentic heart to squeeze through. These days her home is in Tempe, Arizona, where she craves the monsoon scent of creosote and the springtime scent of orange blossoms. When she's not writing books, she can often be found discussing the meaning of life with her daughters, eating her spouse's unrivaled culinary creations, sitting in circle with wild-hearted friends, or reading a book.

INGRID L. TAYLOR is a poet, essayist, queer animist, and veterinarian. Her work has most recently appeared or is forthcoming in *Poet Lore, Artemis Journal, Black Fox Literary, Southwest Review, Collateral Journal,* and others. She received *Punt Volat Journal's* Annual Poetry Award and is a three-time Pushcart nominee. Her nonfiction has appeared in *HuffPost, Sentient Media,* and *Feminist Food Journal.* She has been awarded support for her writing from the Pentaculum Artist Residency, Playa Artist Residency, the Horror Writers Association, the Right to Write fellowship, and Gemini Ink. Find out more about her work at ingridltaylor.com and on Instagram @tildybear.

VANESSA ROWAN WHITFIELD is a Celtic-American author currently living in the east of the States. The ecofeminist writer enjoys scribing poems of all forms, short stories, and personal narratives inspired by her time living off the land as a wildling on various communes, and healing through nature. Her work has been published in various literary magazines and has been shared in galleries and on local television, international radio, and podcasts. A gentle recluse, the award-winning poet can often be found in a garden, channeling inspiration. Her work and publications can be viewed on her Instagram @Nessanthemum.

LIZ KELNER POZEN is an artist and retired psychotherapist living in Boston. Her paintings have been exhibited in galleries across the US, and she has authored two books of poetry and painting, *The Heart of the Family* and *Salami*, as well as a children's book, *The What Ifs*. Her poetry has also been published in *pluck!*, *Metonym*, *River and South Review*, *Stories That Need to Be Told 2021*, and by MassPoetry. Pozen has always been interested in individual psychology and family dynamics. In her work she explores the beauty, complexity, and drama of everyday life.

MARIE A. UNINI is a writer and certified Wayfinder life coach. Her nonfiction short work "The Raven" was published by the University of Texas Press, in the anthology *What Wildness Is This: Women Write About the Southwest*, in 2006, and her one-act play, *Those Hopscotch People*, about one mother and daughter's end-of-life journey, was produced by the Antelope Valley College One-Act Play Festival in 2004. Marie has been journaling, photographing, and writing memoir of her travels, family, and important others her entire adult life, most voluminously in the last twenty-five years. She figures it's about time to get a little bit more of it out into the world of readers. Marie lives in Juniper Hills, California, a rural high desert community in Los Angeles County, lying on the northern face of the San Gabriel Mountain range, with her artist husband Bob, Calypso the mellow gelding, and Miss Piggy the voracious mare.

ELISE BALL is an artist and writer currently residing in southern Appalachia. She is an MFA candidate in poetry at Queens University of Charlotte, where she also works as an editorial assistant for *Qu*, a literary magazine.

ARMEN BACON is the author of three books: *Griefland: An Intimate Portrait of Love, Loss and Unlikely Friendship* and *My Name Is Armen* (vols. I and II). Her essays have appeared in Maria Shriver's *Architects of Change*, *Entropy*, *Brevity Blog*, *Hybred Magazine*, *Streetlight Magazine* (her collaborative essay "Water" received third prize, July 2021), and the *Fresno Bee*. She was a guest artist for the CSU Summer Arts Program (July 2022) and is currently working on a new book project, "Daring to Breathe."

KARLA K. MORTON, *omnium curiositatum explorator*, has fifteen books, with *The National Parks: A Century of Grace* most historic—there's no other poetry book written in situ from each of the sixty-two US national parks to culturally preserve and protect the parks for the next seven generations. Morton gives a percentage of royalties back to the national parks. She's published in *American Life in Poetry*, *Alaska Quarterly Review*, *Southword*, *Arkansas Review*, *Atlanta Review*, *Lascaux Review*, *New Ohio Review*, and many others. A Western Wrangler Heritage Award Winner, E2C grant recipient, two-time Indie National Book Award Winner, and short-listed for the International Rubery Book Prize, she's nominated for the National Cowgirl Hall of Fame and was named Texas Poet Laureate in 2010.

LILA QUINN is a poet and performer from rural Missouri. She earned her MFA in creative writing from the University of Wisconsin–Madison in 2015. She now lives in Boulder, Colorado.

MOLLY AKIN is a writer based in coastal Massachusetts. A Kansas City native, she explored the world as an "unschooled" teenager before earning a BFA from School of the Museum of Fine Arts at Tufts University and an MA from Harvard University Extension School. Her work is informed by her experiences as a woman, mother, and person living with invisible disabilities. She is currently working on her first chapbook with the support of a 2023 Pandemic Recovery Grant from the Massachusetts Cultural Council.

SARAH SCHIFF earned her PhD in contemporary American literature from Emory University but is a fugitive from higher education. She now writes fiction and teaches high school English in Atlanta. Her stories have appeared in the *Saturday Evening Post, Cleaver, Raleigh Review, J Journal*, and *MonkeyBicycle*, among others. One story has also been nominated for a Pushcart Prize. Wouldn't you know it: she's currently at work on a novel.

JESS WHETSEL is a writer, editor, and public speaker based in Toledo, Ohio. She also works as a farmhand on a local flower farm, a job that connects her to the land and brings her great joy. She received her BA in English/creative writing and German in 2010 from Denison University, and her master's in social work in 2017 from the University of Denver. Since then, her work life has been eclectic in nature, but she has always returned to writing; poetry was her first love and will forever be her creative home. You can find her online at www.jesswhetsel.com, or follow her on Instagram @jesswhetselwrites.

JOANNA ZARKADAS has been practicing "random acts of writing" ever since she could hold a pencil. Her poetry and prose have been published in many venues. Besides spending time with her granddaughter, her favorite thing to do is to read her work out loud to live audiences. On her seventieth birthday seventy people came to hear her one-woman show. Currently she is working on a memoir in verse.

Made in the USA
Las Vegas, NV
17 October 2023